Other books by R. D. Lawrence

Wildlife in Canada (1966)
The Place in the Forest (1967)
Where the Water Lilies Grow (1968)
The Poison Makers (1969)
Cry Wild (1970)
Maple Syrup (1971)
Wildlife in North America: Mammals (1974)
Wildlife in North America: Birds (1974)

Illustrated by Bill Elliott

Alfred A. Knopf
New York
1977

PADDY

A Naturalist's Story of an Orphan Beaver

R.D. Lawrence

THIS IS A BORZOI BOOK
PUBLISHED BY ALFRED A. KNOPF, INC.

Copyright © 1977 by R. D. Lawrence
Illustrations copyright © 1977 by Bill Elliott

LIBRARY OF CONGRESS CATALOGING IN PUBLICATION DATA
Lawrence, R. D.   [date]   Paddy.
1. Beavers.   2. Natural history—Ontario.   I. Title.
QL737.R632L38   1977   599'.3232   76–39964
ISBN 0–394–40403–3

MANUFACTURED IN THE UNITED STATES OF AMERICA
FIRST EDITION

To my wife, Sharon, and to my amanuensis,
Lorraine Lowe, gratefully . . .

One It was late May. The sun was warm, the grasses lush and green, and the water lilies peeped from the lake surface, their blooms not yet fully open to the new season. It was evening, almost; but there was still enough sunshine to make the land glow and to warm its creatures and to highlight the cloverleaf outline of the small wilderness lake that sat placid within its rocky cup.

On a continent so bountifully endowed with lakes of majestic size and depth, this little body of water tucked snugly into a wrinkle of Precambrian granite was but a spit droplet, an insignificant little pan of water not worthy of cartographic identity. It was just one of the many thousands of water holes that dot the face of North America from the borders of Mexico to the edges of the Arctic Barrens. All the same, it was important to me that evening as I scanned its surface and contours with field glasses from my perch near the crown of a tall white pine. I had spent three laborious days searching for it, pushing my canoe through marshes and swamps, following innumerable creeks and streams that until now had always led me in the opposite direction to the one that I knew I must take. Now I had found it; I had not, after all, been chasing a will-o'-the-wisp conjured by an old man's imagination, as I had been beginning to fear.

Old Alec had been right, I thought, as I looked at the grubby map that he had penciled for me on one side of a greasy brown paper bag: "Ven you see it, you vill know it right away, by Yesuss," he had told me almost seven years earlier as we sat sipping aquavit in the little frame cottage he had put up with his own hands on an abandoned farmstead some eight miles from International Falls, Minnesota.

I had accepted the proffered map and glanced at the shaky pencil lines politely, but without any real interest, humoring the old man and little dreaming that one day I would follow the scrawled directions drawn from memory and find the lake near which he had built his first log cabin.

Old Alec's real name was Elof Fenstrum, but nobody had called him that for fifty years or more, and even before then he had been called plain Alec. He got his nickname because of the way his Swedish tongue pronounced the words "I like," which emerged, even when I met him, as "Ah lek," an expression that he used frequently.

At the time he drew the map for me he was eighty-six years old, a tall, gaunt man with a thousand wrinkles seaming his face and setting off deep blue eyes and a shock of snow-white hair; a vigorous octogenarian who was an avowed bachelor and "did for himself" with fierce independence and cantankerous determination. He had been born in a fishing village near Gävle, Sweden, on the Gulf of Bothnia, in 1869. He toiled and suffered there for the first eighteen years of his life, until he had managed to scrape together enough money to afford steerage passage on an immigrant ship that left Stockholm for New York in the summer of 1887. After buying his rail ticket to Beaudette, Minnesota, where an uncle he had never known was to meet him, Old Alec had "four dollars American" left from his meager savings.

"Yesuss Christ, though. I sure vas hongry on that trip!" he told me, and I could almost hear his voice that evening as I perched in the tall pine and looked at his map and remembered the brief but strong friendship that developed between us following a chance encounter in a hardware store in International Falls. Now he was dead and I was following his old trail and I half expected to see his tall figure trudging to his cabin loaded with the beaver pelts that had brought him to this place in 1906.

I put the map into my pocket and continued to study the lake through the glasses. As I watched, I heard the ribald yelling of a loon, but the bird remained out of sight; three black ducks moved out from the shallows on the south bank of the lake and swam lazily along, now and then dipping their glossy green heads as they searched for food on the bottom. Then I saw two beaver; they were adult animals, swimming in line astern, their heads and part of their forequarters raised high out of the water as they inspected their country after emerging from the lodge. Their home was a big one, built on the edge of a small island that stuck out of the water close to the shore in the eastern "leaf" of the lake, the only one I could see from the pine tree. Quietly they swam toward a cattail swamp where I presumed they were going to feed, once they had made sure that it was safe to do so.

My sentiments at that moment were mixed. I was elated because I was here and I had four months of freedom ahead of me to devote to the study of beaver, an animal which had in recent years exerted tremendous fascination for me and which I consider to be the most extraordinary mammal in North America; but I was a little sad also, because I remembered Old Alec so vividly and I realized for the first time how much the old man had loved this out-of-the-way corner of wilderness where he had spent five lonely years. I regretted that I had not initially shared his enthusiasm for this beaver country about which he had never tired of talking. Now I felt as though he had left me this country as an inheritance; an illusion, of course, because this was government land in the Province of Ontario, situated less than two hundred miles from the city of Toronto and about eleven hundred miles away from the place where Old Alec and I had met.

I was busy with these thoughts as I scrambled down the tree and jumped onto the moss-covered rock at its base, but the need to make camp for the night forced me to attend to more practical things and to leave my memories and fancies for later, when in the comfort of the tent I could lull myself to sleep thinking of the man and the knowledge he had imparted to me.

I retraced my steps to where I had left the canoe in the shelter of a large clump of willows that grew at the edge of the last marsh I had traversed. I must pitch the tent, gather firewood, and cook supper, then I could relax and plan for the morning. In truth, I still had a great deal to do before I could settle down to my beaver study. I had found Old Alec's Lake, as I immediately christened it, but I had not yet discovered a water route into it or the place where the old cabin had been built. No doubt by this time it was just a pile of rotting wood fibers, but from the old man's description of the area, this would be the place to set up my base camp. By now, because I had found the lake, I trusted his memory and his map and I was sure I would find the small spring of clear water that he had carefully marked near the cabin site.

I dragged the canoe farther up the bank and automatically half-hitched the bow line to one of the willow trees; then I started unpacking my gear while my mind was busy computing what my eyes had seen from the pine tree. I estimated that the lake was about a mile and a half from the tall pine, and I was nearly sure that the big marsh I had crossed to reach the rocky hummocks where the pine trees grew was fed by water escaping from the lake. The problem was to select the right channel from among the many that the beaver had cut to allow them safe passage to their feeding grounds, for these waterways went helter-skelter in all directions.

I pondered over this as I collected rocks, made a hearth ring, and kindled a fire, using deadfall maple that burned cleanly and would soon develop enough heat to fry some bacon and warm up some canned beans. With the last slices of bread that remained from a loaf I had brought with me, I would make toast over the coals—the best kind of toast in the world! This would be my supper tonight, and coffee, of course. Simple fare, but delicious after a hard day's journey, spiced as it would be by the faint taste of wood smoke.

After balancing the battered coffeepot on a rock where it was licked by the flames, I cut slices off the slab of bacon and put them into the cast-iron frying pan, a heavy utensil, but one that more than made up for its weight by its efficiency and durability. As the bacon sizzled in the pan, I took another look at Old Alec's map, going over it once more to get a clearer picture of the country ahead.

While I was up the tree I used the other side of the map to make a rough sketch of the lake and of the country surrounding it, marking my estimate of the distance to various landmarks and tracing the route of the shallow valleys that lay between the rock outcrops. I turned the map over and looked at my work. From where I sat, the marsh ran sharply eastward and followed a valley that was about a quarter of a mile wide and appeared to lead directly to the lake; I estimated I would have to travel about a mile through this lowland before gaining access to open water.

Experience had taught me the wisdom of weighing my supplies before I set out into the wilderness and I knew that my canoe, packed, contained 110 pounds of gear; add to that my own 150 pounds and the canoe's 60 pounds of empty weight and I had a gross lading of 320 pounds. This was a fair load, but I felt it should be possible to paddle and pole the laden canoe through the reeds until I reached the lake, and once I was settled there, I could return in the empty canoe with ax and bush knife and clear a regular passage to the main part of the marsh, where the beaver channels were wider and the going was a lot easier. This would assure me of an easy exit whenever I had to go to the outside for supplies.

Because of the many detours I had been forced to make during the last three days, I had absolutely no idea how far I had traveled from the county road where I had left my four-wheel-drive station wagon, but I thought I could retrace my route, following my back trail, in half a day and do better than that once I became fully acquainted with the country.

I sat that evening enjoying my supper and trying to keep down the excitement that I felt at the prospects of exploring Old Alec's Lake and I remember that I had to be firm with myself in order to curb my impatience, now that I was so near to my goal; an impatience that urged me to keep on going tonight, right after I had eaten. This would have been foolish, of course, and I knew it; the chances of my finding the lake in the dark were remote indeed, but although I was able to control the impulse, forcing myself to do the sensible thing and stay the night in this place, I was very restless and most anxious to reach the lake and settle down to my field studies.

By eight o'clock I had finished my meal and put away the maps and washed the dishes; the tent was pitched and my two food packs were hanging from the branchy white pine under which I was camped, high enough from the ground to be out of reach of raccoons—public enemy number one of food packs—and black bears.

Afterward, I settled to a quiet pipe beside the glowing fire, puffing thoughtfully and letting my gaze be drawn into the red heart of the coals, feeling as always contentment from the warmth and the strange, hypnotic effect that the flickering of open flames seems to exert upon the mind. The hardwood burned cleanly and without the fussy crackling of pine, producing little blue flames that danced in turn as they rose and fell in different parts of the hearth, while the twinkling coals constantly changed their intensity and color as each absorbed oxygen from the air. For some time it was as though only my mind and the fire existed in the darkness of the wilderness night. Each had become attuned to the other, two forces able in some mysterious fashion to bridge the gap between first man crouching outside his cave and modern man seeking to rediscover the secrets of creation. "Pyrophilosophy" is the term I have coined for this fascinating sort of communion that can, on occasion, keep me in a state of semi-trance for a considerable time.

That night the spell was broken soon after it began. A loon was responsible. The bird started its madcap hallooing from somewhere within the denseness of the marsh, the cadences of its song rising in the darkness accompanied by the sound of the bird's rapid movements as it dashed exuberantly over the surface. It was a solo performance and it ended quickly, probably because no other loons joined in for the prolonged session of delirious cackle that these divers are so fond of.

When the loon quieted I looked up at the sky and lost

myself again for a time as I found Ursa Major and followed its pointers to Polaris in a firmament that was like blue-black velvet sprinkled liberally with sequins. No moon, but a beautiful night during one of my favorite months. May offers so much in the wilderness, particularly in the more northerly parts of our continent, which, after a prolonged period of cold, thaw slowly through April while new life prepares itself for more robust emergence during the following month. May is the time of young leaves and of blossoms, of new grasses and colorful wildflowers, of small golden bees essaying hesitant flights to gather nectar sparingly; young animals are newly populating the land, some just puling little mites, naked and blind in their dens, others more lusty, furred and adventurous as they force direction in wobbly limbs; the birds sing joyously and display the fullness of courting colors. The wilderness, one feels, comes fully and gloriously alive. But the hordes of blood-sucking insects have not yet marshaled; true, during warm sunny days the advance guards of mosquitoes and black-flies buzz or whisk through the air and take a sip or two from the exposed parts of the body, but I never begrudge them their bloody drinks then, because they are themselves feed for many of the returned birds and I know that the coolness that comes with sundown will drive the insects to seek warmth and shelter under low-lying leaves and grass blades, leaving the darkness for undisturbed enjoyment and contemplation. And so it was that night: cold enough for grateful acceptance of the fire, but warm enough to allow the body to remain still without undue discomfort to those parts that faced away from the heat.

I was still gazing at the heavens when a beaver pounded water with its paddle tail not more than twenty yards from the shore and the sound was so loud and so totally unexpected that it startled me, made me jump unwittingly. In response to my sudden movement came a second tail splash and I heard the soft rippling that followed it as the beaver dived for bottom. Knowing something of the habits of the beaver by then, I was aware that the animal must have risen to the surface, noted my light and the fire, and come quietly to investigate this newness in its domain; but because it could not determine what manner of creature squatted unmoving beside the strange nightlight, it had slapped water. My startled movement revealed an unknown, but large animal to the beaver's eyes and it slapped once more as it dived.

This incident reminded me that most observers appear to have inaccurately interpreted the beaver's habit of slapping its tail on the water. The widely held theory is that the animal makes the sound primarily as a warning to other beaver, and this, I contend, is not so. That night I held the view—which I have since confirmed, at least to my own satisfaction—that the beaver's noisy action is undertaken for two different, but related reasons: to startle for the purpose of identification *and* to startle for the purpose of escape. In either event, the sudden, sharp report made by the paddle-like tail contacting the water surface is calculated to surprise an enemy and put it off balance long enough for the beaver to recognize it or, if need be, to escape.

I do agree that the sound made by the tail slap serves as a warning for other beaver in the *immediate area*, which have learned by observation to become alert when one of their number pounds water, but their alarm reaction is, I believe, a side effect and not the main purpose of the slap. Thus, in certain circumstances, if a swimming beaver fails to quickly identify some unusual object or movement in or around its pond, it becomes instantly cautious and curious. The unknown must become known, but identity must be established from the safety of the water.

With a lightning reflex movement, the beaver slaps water. Ker-splat! The report is sharp and loud, and even before the water droplets generated by the splash have had time to fall back into the pond, the beaver has raised its shoulders and head the better to see, hear, and smell. If it is still unsure, it will probably slap once or twice more; if uncertainty remains, it may dive slowly or it may swim quietly away.

One might suppose the beaver to be wise enough to dive immediately upon being confronted with a doubtful situation, but such a supposition would not take into account the very many times during normal wilderness living that a beaver—or any other wild animal, for that matter—is faced with uncertainty while still having to pursue life as calmly and efficiently as possible. If instant panic resulted on each occasion when it was confronted by the unknown, a beaver would spend practically all of its time submerged or in its lodge, unable to feed properly and soon to die a victim of its own fears.

When a beaver meets a recognized enemy, or some very startling event, such as a man in a canoe, it dives immediately and slaps its tail as it is going down. *But,* with the exception of man traveling upon the water in a boat, I find it difficult to accept that beaver ever face real danger while swimming in their pond or lake, because their main natural predators—wolves, cougars, wolverines, coyotes, lynxes, bobcats, and bears—are not likely to enter the water in chase of such a champion diver and swimmer unless the beaver happens to be very close to shore in shallow water; an otter or a large mink will undoubtedly attack a beaver kit if they can catch one away from its mother, but I do not think this threat is significant enough to have developed the tail-slapping habit.

I believe that the beaver essentially slaps the water to identify a *shore* object, be that man or beast, but it does so only when it intends to land for feeding.

Significantly, a beaver makes no attempt to thump its broad tail on land, which I would expect it to do if this action was designed as a warning to other beaver. Ashore, the animal is a slow and clumsy runner and easy prey for any predator that can manage to sneak up on it, though it is difficult to surprise a beaver on land; its eyes are not very keen, but it more than makes up for this deficiency by having extremely acute hearing and a highly developed sense of smell.

The hooting of a horned owl reached into my mind and switched it back to the bush night. I listened to the five distinct *whoo* notes that were repeated after a short pause, and immediately afterward I noted the silence of the little things that had been scuttling through last year's dead grasses and leaves before the hunting bird sang its tremolo. The gentle rustling of their progress had been picked up by my subconscious in the same way that the crackling of the fire and the sluggish movement of the marsh water had been tuned in; but now that the pattering mice and voles had stilled their feet in fearful response to the owl's call, the absence of their movements was more detectable than the small noises that they had been making.

I often wonder what it is about the wilderness that is able to sharpen senses blunted by civilization. In a city, with its constant mechanical clangors, nuances of sound go unnoticed; in the wild, the smallest noise registers, even though one may not be consciously aware of it until it has ceased. This "sixth sense" awareness is intriguing on its own account, but sometimes, as was the case that night, it proves of definite value to a naturalist.

The owl's call, and the way that the mice and voles had reacted to it, reminded me of the interrelationship of life and made me realize that I had been a little too single-minded in my desire to learn more about the beaver. I was so eager to study this animal that I had been in danger of excluding all else from my quest, as though I had set out for some zoo to watch beaver in the sterility of a cement pond. Now I could again see the country in its proper perspective, an intricate blend of life, color, and sound of which the beaver was a part, but not an isolated whole. True, the beaver must occupy the point of focus, but no definitive study of one animal can be undertaken without consideration of the influences exerted by its environment and by the other life forms that share it; the land had to be studied as a whole, every action and reaction had to be observed, plotted, and, if possible, interpreted.

This, as far as I was aware, was beaver country untouched by man for more than half a century, a land unmolested and untrapped, where nature was yet able to maintain her balance. To "get it all together," I must become a part of the country. I must learn to react like the animals that I was going to study and I must try, as best I could, to *feel* the very soul of the wilderness. And, finally, I had to attempt to think like a beaver, to put myself in that animal's place without allowing anthropomorphism to cloud my judgments.

On the heels of these thoughts came uncertainty and a premature sense of failure. Could I, indeed, sublimate my instincts to the degree of fineness needed? Would the land and its animals accept me as a harmless part of their world? As I extinguished the fire with water from the marsh, self-doubts were heavy in my mind. I turned from stirring the soaked ashes and entered the tent, undressed, and crawled into my sleeping bag. Soon I was sound asleep.

Two

At first I thought that a vivid dream had awakened me, but a moment or two after I opened my eyes within the darkened tent, I heard the long, melancholy howl of the timber wolf. The call was repeated five times, from nearby, and filled the forest night with its nerve-tingling cadences until its echoes were lost in space; then an absolute stillness followed. I got the impression that the forest and its creatures were waiting for another burst of song from the wild dog, as though the primordial howls had the power to bring silence to the wilderness and to cause all other forms of life to lie unmoving and submissive to the will of the wolf.

Such is the fallacy of human reason! I had superimposed my own feelings upon the reality of wilderness life, awed despite myself, even though I had been touched often by the lonely song of the wolf. Actually it was I who lay unmoving and silent, holding my breath, awaiting a fresh series of howls. Outside the tent, once I rid myself of these fancies, I could hear the forest life progressing normally.

Now I was wide awake. I groped for the flashlight and shone its beam on my watch. It was four-thirty and too early to rise yet, but I could not go back to sleep because, as always, I had become too fascinated by the beautiful, haunting melody in the wolf's voice, wanting to hear it again and discovering new interest in my own reactions to it. Even though there was at least one more hour before first light, I decided to get up and dress and light a fire and make coffee.

For a time, I just sat huddled over the blaze, warming my hands on the mug and listening to the wilderness night, not thinking very much, half expecting to hear the wolf again; but when a beaver rose to the surface and came to inspect my campfire, then slapped its tail three times in quick succession before it dived again, I began to think about the strange rodent that had brought me to this place and that had for so long fascinated me.

It may be that the wolf howl drew me into the mists of prehistory, but even before the sound of the beaver's last splash was stilled, I was trying to imagine what this country must have been like in the days when the North American beaver grew to be larger than a present-day black bear and scaled over seven hundred pounds, as fossil remains indicate. What a creature this must have been! This giant ancestor of the modern beaver was building huge dams and cutting down enormous primeval trees while the saber-toothed tiger prowled hungrily around the edges of its great ponds and the mastodon still trampled over our continent.

As the centuries passed and the face of North America became modified, the exuberant, exaggerated life forms of the Pleistocene began to reduce their size and sharpen their specialized modes of living. Many of the beaver's companion animals, such as the saber-toothed tiger and the mastodon and the sloth and the giant vulture, were unable to change and eventually became extinct, but the tenacious rodent hung on. Its food supplies, though remaining abundant, were drastically reduced in size. The lumbering giant had to work a lot harder in order to stay alive, and it probably burned up almost as much energy in food gathering as it needed in order to maintain its body's metabolism. This was the most likely cause of its change in size, for though the beaver managed to cling to life, succeeding generations of its kind, born, in effect, undernourished, were unable to match the proportions of their ancestor. Eventually, when beaver and forest growth reached a point of size balance, the rodent stopped getting smaller and today, when seemingly stable growth conditions exist, the beaver and its food supplies keep pace with each other, at least superficially. In fact, the ungainly rodent has never stopped trying to attain giant size, being the only mammal that keeps growing right up to its time of death. In theory, if a modern beaver lived long enough, it could possibly reach the great size of its prehistoric forebears. The longer a beaver lives, the bigger it gets, and this accounts for the wide variations in size encountered in adult beavers.

The fire died down and the morning chill drew me out of my reverie and prompted me to reach for fresh wood to nourish the coals into flames. The stars had paled and the green-blue light of dawn gave some substance to the forest and to the outline of the pond just as the birds, particularly the ducks, greeted the new day with their own special voices.

I stood up and stretched and walked toward the water to get the kinks out of my limbs; then I stood facing the east and watched as new light filtered over the land.

Dawn during fine weather is always an exciting time in any habitat, whether a city, a section of farmland, or an area of wilderness such as the one in which I traveled; there is the magic of the timeless sun as it creeps over the eastern horizon, there is the music of the birds and the smell of land that is newly awakening.

At first the delicate color arises pale pink, like fine gauze across the distant skyline, then shades of orange and mauve and gold herald the coming of the sun, which soon arcs bold and fire-bright over the tree line. As a day is born, the land and its life forms respond to it, each in their own ways.

Outside the tent it was crisp and cool and as I zippered my bush jacket I faced the panorama of rising color and enjoyed it as much that day as I did the very first time I witnessed it with full awareness almost thirty years earlier, when after a restless night I left my bed and went to a window in time to see the dawn break over the chimney pots of London and to notice how it coaxed playful reflections from the waters of the dour river Thames. I shall always remember my first conscious sunrise, for it put beauty into an otherwise squalid landscape and made me see England's ancient capital with new eyes.

Similarly, on that morning in marsh country, the breaking day with its kaleidoscopic colors gave me a new perspective on the tangled, obstacle-ridden country that had hitherto seemed intent upon foiling my purpose. Yesterday the marsh was a troublesome barrier between me and Old Alec's Lake; today it acquired personality and character and it made me aware that though it was unruly it was also the guardian of the lake, slowing the escape of water and by its very unruliness preventing the invasion of the lakeland by unscrupulous members of my own species.

By the time I had formulated these thoughts, the sun had revealed itself fully and as I continued to look at the day I saw a turkey vulture come gliding in from the south, approaching low enough to show the details of its six-foot wings with their finger-like tips spread wide to help stabilize the great black bird as it rode the thermals with magnificent ease. I watched it spiral over the marsh, then begin to climb, rising effortlessly until it became a black dot and finally disappeared.

When it was gone I breakfasted, taking my time, sitting on a rock and studying the area with care and making mental notes of the landmarks that would be useful during those occasions when I retraced my route to the outside. Time passed all too quickly in this way and it was not until a white-throated sparrow came to perch on a nearby pine and regale the morning with its flute-like song that I became aware of the lateness of the hour.

The little bird's voice drew my gaze upward and after I spotted the songster I noted that the sun had climbed high and I realized that I had delayed longer than I intended. When I got up to dismantle the camp, the white-throat flitted away and as I packed the canoe his beautiful voice reached me again, not as close this time, but just as enjoyable.

A short while later I was ready to leave, but first I took time to cut a ten-foot push pole to help me fight the marsh. I chose a straight, two-inch poplar, axed it down and trimmed off its main branches; then I cut off the tender top and threw it into the water for the beaver to enjoy, and after stowing the long pole into the sixteen-foot canoe, I boarded and pushed away from the shore.

Ten minutes later the warmth of the sun encouraged me to take off my shirt, not because I was hot, but because I find pleasure in the touch of the wind and the sunlight on my bare skin and I seem better able to feel nature like that, to absorb the events of the wildwoods and to attune to their sounds, as though naked contact with the elements has the power to bridge the gap between modern civilization with its attendant strictures and the abandoned freedoms inherent in the world of nature.

For an hour I followed the twisting course of the beaver canal and at the end of that time I was pleased to note that the water was still deep enough for easy paddling and the channel wide enough to allow me to move along without brushing into the walls of cattails.

Then the main channel ended. Three secondary openings faced me. Which one to take? Each canal was just a little wider than the canoe and none of them appeared to go in the desired direction; yet any one of the openings, or even all three, could suddenly turn and lead me to the lake. To help me decide which one to take, I tested the outflow of water from the lake.

Paddling to turn the bows into the wall of cattails so as to anchor the canoe in one place, I broke off three pieces of dry stem, each about two inches long, and threw one into the mouth of each watercourse and timed their progress toward the canoe, reasoning that the outgoing lake water might flow faster along the canal that led more directly to the source of the current. The reeds moved very slowly, but the piece from the left-hand channel was just a little faster than the others. Into its course I turned the canoe.

The going became more difficult and I had to hold the paddle almost perpendicular to the gunwale in order to keep the blade clear of the reeds. And I had to put my shirt back on because the cattails were closing in over my head and scraping against my body and showering me with bits of dried leaf, pollen dust, various tiny insects, and spider webs. I was glad that some whim had prompted me to wear my broad-brimmed canvas hat instead of my favorite orange cap, though the physical irritations were minor compared to the directional confusion created by the twists and turns I was forced to make.

In a large marsh such as the one through which I traveled, the channels form a series of waterways that can vary considerably in width and length; some are short and narrow, muskrat-built openings; others are wide and long and winding, swaths cut through the reeds by the combined efforts of beaver and current. Unless a traveler knows the country, or has definite landmarks as guides, it is quite possible to wander through such mazes for a long time, and on more than one occasion I have slept in my canoe when darkness forbade further travel. Such experiences are not necessarily dreadful, but they are uncomfortable enough to avoid if possible.

Soon after entering the narrow channel, visibility was reduced to a few yards in any direction and only the dry rustling of my own progress broke the stillness. When I had been in the tunnel of cattails for an hour and a half I began to get irritable. Pushing through the labyrinth was hot work, little itchy things were sticking to my sweaty body, and I was bothered by the knowledge that I would have considerable trouble should I decide to try and turn the canoe around if I was forced to go back and seek another channel; and the alternative to turning the craft was moving my load of gear from the bows to the stern, so that I could change places and paddle forward.

I kept moving as best I could. Soon I put away the paddle and used the pole. The going was easier in the straight places, but to negotiate some of the sharper bends I had to drop the pole and use the paddle, or pull the boat around by grabbing the cattails. In this way almost another hour went by and I was seriously thinking about turning back, even if I had to sit on top of my gear, when it seemed to me that the canal was getting wider. I pushed more heartily with the pole and after traveling about four more canoe lengths I saw uninterrupted blue sky and the boat no longer touched the sides of the channel. Five minutes later I was able to paddle again and in another ten minutes I came out of the tunnel into an area of open water. As I paused to look around, a small flock of black ducks winged sibilantly overhead, losing height rapidly as the birds headed in what I fervently hoped was the direction of the lake. The ducks, I thought, would confirm my hope: if I heard them land on open water, I could be certain that the lake was near. I listened. In about twenty seconds the clear sounds of their splashdown became audible, and in another moment the ducks began to gossip. Old Alec's Lake was not far away!

Ahead of me appeared the opening of a solitary channel and, guided by the voices of the ducks, I paddled into it. Ten minutes later I cleared the marsh and found the lake. The black ducks took wing when I appeared; a beaver swimming toward the cattails slapped his tail and dived. I gave a couple of hard strokes and then let the canoe drift while I rested and looked around and noted at one point that I was gliding over a flooded dam; it made me realize that there might be others in this area that were also underwater as a result of the heavy spring runoff.

Oriented by the map, it took me only fifteen minutes to cross the lake and locate Old Alec's cabin near the place where the stream ran briskly out of a fissure in the face of a steep rock outcrop. The water was icy cold and over the years had eroded a channel for itself that twisted and turned for about a hundred yards before it entered a shallow basin and escaped into the lake.

The cabin was as I expected to find it, rotten, partly collapsed, and the home of mice and squirrels. The south part had managed to resist some of the assaults of weather and time, but the whole thing heeled precariously under the weight of the sagging roof. A small window in the only wall that stood fully upright offered entrance and I climbed over the rotting sill and looked around inside. The old man's bed frame was nailed to one wall; it was a rude affair of cedar poles that had once been webbed with canvas, and although the mattress was long gone, a few wisps of vegetable fibers still clung to the frame. A shelf above the bed survived. On it I found an almost entirely rusted oil lamp and a pair of pliers so badly oxidized they were seized solid; beside these things was an empty bottle without a label that was thick with grime and cobwebs. I took these items and put them outside, keepsakes, and when I turned around again, I saw an ax that Old Alec must have forgotten; the handle had been gnawed by porcupines and the blade was pitted and chipped, but I put it with the other things. There was nothing else of interest in the flimsy shack, and as I took one last look at its interior, the faint hope of repairing it that I had entertained faded completely; the building would soon collapse. It was unsafe to linger in there.

Outside again, I walked to the canoe and began to unpack, taking my gear to a site not far from the cabin where a big white pine offered shade and a screen of young spruces sheltered a nice, level piece of ground on which to pitch the tent. Later I collected rocks for a hearth rin~ a. . then I made a fire and had lunch, after which I sorte my gear and tidied up. Canned goods were stacked inside the tent with tools, clothing, and sleeping bag; perishable food went into the packsacks, which I hung from a branch.

All was now shipshape about the camp and as I turned away from the branch the empty canoe lying upside down on the rocky "beach" suggested a tour of the lake. I walked the forty yards from the tent to the shoreline and righted the boat and put it into the water; then I pushed off and glided away.

Fifty yards from shore I let the canoe drift while I looked at the landscape. Above me, the blue sky was cloudless and aglow with benign sunshine; around me stretched the ageless wilderness filled with the birds and the animals and the insects and the trees and the plants and the flowers. I listened to the vibrant day song of the forest and I looked upon the array of flashing colors. In the reeds from which I had earlier emerged, the voices of the ducks were husky and soft, while in the air the songs of the birds and the buzzing of the flies could not quite subdue the murmur of young leaves rubbing against one another. Spring beckoned that afternoon and I willingly responded to its signals, but I also felt sorrow for Old Alec, because he would have loved to be here to share his lake with me.

Then I realized that sadness was the wrong emotion, for the old man had lived a full and useful life and had made his exit from it with dignity in a place and manner of his own choosing after giving me his friendship and willing me his lake. There was beauty in the thought.

I knelt in the stern and soaked up the sun, letting my mind romp free and allowing my gaze to fall upon whatever took its fancy. I was at peace, a man-animal alone in his original setting and too busy observing and feeling to have need of companionship; indeed, not wanting the society of my own kind and preferring this gentle loneliness that allowed me to attend fully to my own thoughts.

The sun sucked vapor from the water and it danced and shimmered and projected a few small mirages that were magically suspended in the air and somehow accentuated the shine of the sun while distorting the shapes of the reeds: heat haze, impish curtain of sun energy seeking to escape into space. Quite suddenly the sleek head of a beaver emerged upon the surface of the lake, lingered for a moment or two, and submerged once more; then it popped up two hundred yards ahead of the canoe, its arrival followed by a slight heaving of the water surface immediately around the swimmer.

The beaver seemed nervous, yet it was curious and I wondered if I had interrupted the animal's patrol of its lake world; or perhaps it had merely come up to swim a little, to take a lazy airing on the sunny surface, and then, if the spirit moved it, to submerge again and return to its lodge. I felt that there was no telling what it was going to do at that moment. It seemed drawn toward the canoe despite itself, hesitating, but nevertheless making an unhurried turn, steering with its tail and kicking with its webbed back feet. It circled the boat, ears pricked, shoulders and head just a little raised. It moved closer to the fat red thing that had suddenly appeared on the lake, then it slapped water, once, pause; twice, pause; three times. Nothing happened; the intruding shape continued floating gently, there was no sudden movement, and the beaver circled once more. It was watchful and strangely daring, but it turned at last, aiming toward the big marsh at the western end of the lake, and it submerged. At first its body was a dark blur under the water; then it was gone. A string of silver bubbles dotted the surface and its progress could be followed until the distance became too great.

From where I floated in the canoe I had a good view of the big beaver lodge that nestled at one end of the small island. A redwing blackbird was perched on a peeled stick that poked out of the very top of the mound. He was indulging in his showy courting ritual for a demure brown hen that flitted busily on the mainland nearby. The cock bird spread his wings and displayed his gaudy red-and-yellow epaulets, bowed two or three times, tail uplifted, and uttered his gurgly, musical call. The hen, with coy pretense, made as though she was unaware of the male's display, but took good care to keep herself in his view so as not to lose his attention.

Another beaver rose to the surface just a few yards away from the lodge and swam in a straight line toward the western end of the lake. After traveling in full view for about a hundred yards, it dived, and I watched through the glasses the trail of bubbles that marked the swimmer's course; I saw that the animal was going in an almost dead-straight line toward the marsh area from which I had gained access to the lake. I was reminded that at one time I had wondered how beaver are able to find their way with such apparent ease when swimming under the surface—even in broad daylight, pond water is usually brown and debris-laden. With its poor sight and its ears and nostrils useless under the water, there would seem to be little to guide a beaver; however, the animal has a simple and effective means of finding its way, even in pitch darkness, through its underwater world.

It is guided by the long and sensitive guard hairs that sprout through its silken pelt. Each of these hairs is anchored to a tiny, individual muscle that raises or lowers it as needed. The coarse hairs are able to feel the flow of the current, and they transmit continuous impulses to the beaver's nervous system when they are subjected to water pressure. Each hair and each muscle is linked to its own nerve ending, and the sensory signals that reach the beaver's brain are not collectively synchronized. Instead, the hairs on the left side of the animal's body transmit signals to the right side of the brain, and the hairs on the right side of the body register their alert on the left side of the brain. In this way the beaver is able to determine the direction from which the current is flowing. The guard hairs, in fact, respond to the movement of current in much the same way as a weather vane answers to the pressure of wind, allowing the animal to swim blindly under the water. By this means all beaver in a pond are soon alerted when a breach in the dam quickens the flow of water that is being lost downstream.

With this kind of assistance from its guard hairs, a beaver can usually find its way around even in strange waters, much as a woodsman can steer by a compass though he may not know what lies ahead. In a home pond or lake, where a beaver is intimately acquainted with the usual directional flow of the current, the animal hardly has need of vision to find its way around, though in clear water or during full moonlight or strong sunshine, it can orient itself visually.

The heavy coat of guard hairs and a down-soft dressing of underfur keep the animal warm during the coldest winter conditions and comfortably cool during the heat of summer, but the marvelous garment must be carefully groomed each time its owner emerges from the water inside the lodge, or during those occasions when a beaver feels secure enough to sit outside. The pelt has to be combed and dried and re-oiled, and debris such as mud, dirt, and small twigs must be removed. Often a family of beaver will groom each other, nibbling a companion's fur or gently scratching it with skillful front paws.

Leeches, ever present in slow-flowing ponds, plague most beaver, and whenever possible they rid themselves of the blood suckers by biting them off—and sometimes eating them, as I saw two beaver do on separate occasions—or, if the pest has anchored itself on a part of an animal's body out of reach of its mouth, one of its companions will probably remove it during a grooming party.

One might be inclined to think that an animal that lavishes so much attention upon its coat has more than its share of vanity, but practical considerations rather than pride of appearance are behind the frequent groomings. Without the continuous renewal of its body oils, the beaver's fur would not repel water. It would quickly lose its insulation properties, and the animal would suffer from cold and also from heat.

Of course, any creature that is so careful of its fur and has a coat of such consistently good quality is asking for trouble if it allows man to catch sight of it. And trouble is precisely what the beaver got not long after the white man arrived in North

America. By the start of the seventeenth century, Europe was clamoring for the pelt of *Castor*, to be used to make the tall "beaver hats" then in fashion. Durable and fine, the underhair of the beaver is microscopically barbed. This made it ideal material for the manufacture of felt, though in nature the minutely barbed hairs, by locking one with the other, form a soft, impermeable blanket within which are trapped numerous air bubbles that insulate the animal against heat and cold.

White men, motivated by greed rather than by any sense of pioneering adventure, migrated over practically the entire continent in their quest for the coveted beaver fur, all the way from Alaska and northern Canada to Florida and Texas and westward to California. In 1670 the Hudson's Bay Company would trade one pound of tobacco for a large, prime beaver pelt, while a long rifle cost a stack of beaver blankets as high as the gun was long. In less than a quarter of a century— between 1853 and 1877—the Hudson's Bay Company alone shipped some three million beaver skins to England. And there were a number of other fur companies around at the time, each bartering for the riches that a quiet, innocent rodent carried on its back.

After the beaver had disappeared there was little movement to be observed on the lake. On shore, the birds flitted about in search of food, uttering their calls from time to time, but the surface of the water was empty and quiet. Half an hour later I decided to return to camp, drink some dehydrated soup, and turn in, for this had been a long day preceded by others of equal length and challenge.

Three

Fatigue and tension combined to slow me down next morning. I prepared a leisurely breakfast in the warmth of sunshine and campfire, ate bannocks and sipped coffee, and I prescribed my own medicine for the day. After almost ninety-six hours of steady travel through the marshlands my body needed a rest; so did my mind, which had been alternately fretting because I couldn't find Old Alec's Lake and preoccupied with the details of my quest. Now it was time to relax and to enjoy the spring and the wilderness, to be lazy in mind as well as in body.

I looked up at the sun and from its position judged the time to be around nine o'clock, but I wasn't really interested in the hour; not enough so, at any rate, to abandon the lazy comfort of my perch and go to the tent to look at my watch. Sun time was good enough for me then and was to remain so, by and large, for the rest of my stay in that place.

I stretched, yawned, felt wonderfully alive and happy, and I watched a red ant climb up one pant leg and scurry toward my tin plate, its shiny, chitinous body pausing now and then, the glossy head with the horn-like mandibles moving from side to side as the insect obeyed senses that instructed it to find the food that was within reach. Quite quickly it reached the edge of the plate, slithered slightly as it climbed the smooth surface, and then bellied over. A piece of bannock about one quarter inch square was near and the ant seized it, put it down, picked it up again more securely, and turned to leave with the huge load, backtracking along its own scent trail exactly the way it had come; over the lip of the plate, onto my pant leg, along it, down onto the ground, and away toward the colonial nest. Soon, unless I moved, hundreds of the little workers would be crawling up my leg as they followed the trail that the scout had blazed by leaking formic acid as it traveled. I smiled at the retreating ant and emptied the remnants of my breakfast onto the ground. When the workers came, they would not have journeyed in vain.

I washed up, put away the utensils, walked down to the edge of the lake, and scanned the tracks along the shore: raccoon, fox, beaver, mouse, weasel; in the shallows, four freshwater clams sat half buried in the ooze, each reposing after undertaking sluggish night journeys through the sand and mud and leaving their well-defined trails, like lines marked on the bottom with a sharp stick. On land, crushed shells showed where a raccoon had dined last night on less fortunate clams.

My attention was taken away from the shellfish by the

clamor of a flock of jays that were congregated on a finger of land about three hundred yards from where I stood. The spur reached out into the lake for about thirty yards. It was across from me, on the other side of the little bay at the end of which Old Alec had built his cabin. The jays had found something and were quarreling over the booty, screaming at each other, diving down, as quickly flying up to land teetering and unsteady on the alder trees. I decided to walk over and investigate the cause of the commotion.

When I was halfway there, the jays took fright and abandoned the scene of their recent quarrel, screaming as they fled. In a few minutes I saw a large boulder, a rounded rock about six feet high and as many wide, on top of which was a variety of droppings, bits of squirrel-chewed pine cones, and tiny ravaged cones from the alders. Nearby I noticed a disturbance of the ground and of the grass and shrubs. Something had happened in this place, recently.

As I stood beside the boulder I saw the bloodstains, dark and almost black in places, brown in others; I saw pieces of brown fur matted by blood and I noticed the bits of bone and sinew and some scraps of furred hide. A beaver had met its death here. Instantly, all lethargy left me. I stooped over the place where the body had been dismembered and eaten, and I began to note the signs. Bit by bit I traced the sequence of events.

By the boulder, snug against its south face, was the depression in the grass where the wolf had lain in wait; the new grass stems were bruised, some of them broken, while last year's dead growth was matted by the wolf's weight. Big tracks were clear in one place where the ground was soft; they showed how the killer had come up to the boulder and bellied down beside it. About five feet in front of the rock, at the broad base of the spur of land, were the marks left by the wolf's front feet when they hit the ground after the first spring; between the spread pug marks of the front feet were the less distinct tracks the back feet made when they hit the ground and launched the wolf into his second spring. Almost beside the worn beaver pathway, more tracks; again of the front feet, on which the wolf had landed; and the brace marks, showing how the animal had grabbed its victim and pulled back, shaking the beaver's body so that the paddle tail had scraped along the mud and left its own peculiar marks. On a low branch of an alder, brown stains told their own story: the blood from the wolf's victim had sprayed as the great canines bit deeply into the beaver's life. Then the pad marks, going from the place of death to the place of eating. That was the story written plainly on the landscape; a recent story, judging from the state of the blood, from the clear tracks, from the still depressed grasses beside the boulder. Recent, but not as recent as last night— the blood would have kept some of its redness; the grass stems would have been more depressed; the matted fur would have been damp; the piece of hide about four inches long and two inches wide would not have been as dry and leathery and the single milk dug that protruded from it would have yet retained some softness.

I examined the piece of belly skin and gave close attention to the pathetic nipple and to the shriveled swelling around it. Two days ago that piece of skin with its milk breast must have been full, dripping full of the sticky, life-giving fluid; now it was sere and brittle and the young which it should nourish were left starving. Where? I looked up and studied the lake, my eyes straying to the big lodge on the small island; of the six lodges that were on the lake, that one seemed the most likely. It was the largest, the oldest, the one that showed the greatest signs of use: peeled poles floating near it, others tamped into the superstructure, a large area clear of lily pads near its underwater entrance.

My feelings were mixed. I knew with an awful certainty

that a wolf had killed a mother beaver. The kits could not survive without her, they would be condemned to one of the worst deaths imaginable: slow starvation, a death terrible because it was prolonged and only made merciful when dehydration rather than the need for protein made the little beaver die of thirst. For some seconds I felt rage against the killer wolf and I was swearing vengeance on him when the realities of wilderness life brought me up short. I had been about to make a judgment based on human emotions and conditioned by years of civilized rationale. There was no place for that kind of thinking here. Certainly, I felt pity for the kits and sorrow for the mother, but I had sympathy for the wolf, too. He killed to live, as I did, as all things must do, and he had fulfilled his needs two nights ago; a mother beaver had died and her kits were in danger of death. Suddenly, I felt impelled to search for the kits, if it was not already too late, and if I found them, coax them back to life.

I left the death scene and hurried back to camp and to the canoe, which I launched and paddled to the large beaver lodge. Now I was on top of the mound of mud and sticks and I placed one ear against the breathing hole at its crown: nothing. I looked around; there were no signs of life. I tried to peer through the medley of sticks that were not welded together by mud and which allowed air to enter and to leave the lodge chamber, but there was nothing to see between the cracks, only more interlaced sticks for a few inches down, then darkness. I listened again, hoping to hear the mewing of the young, but no sounds reached me.

Back in the canoe, I paddled to all the other lodges and repeated the listening and the looking, but I found nothing. I was convinced that the big lodge was the right place to seek the young, and since I could not hear them, there was only one way to find out if they were still in the chamber; not a good way, not even a certain way, but it might help me find out. I paddled back to the big lodge, anchored the canoe against a smooth part of the island, landed, and stripped off my clothes.

The water was ice cold, murky; my bare feet stirred up ooze and bits of rotting vegetation; twice I cut myself slightly when I stepped on broken clamshells. At last I was in deep enough to swim. I stroked away until I could not touch bottom; then I dived and swam slowly toward where I thought the main lodge entrance would be, the while trying not to feel the cold that enfolded me, and trying not to think about the leeches that I knew were present in the water. It was like swimming through a sort of thin, brown soup and vision was almost useless. The sunlight faded within inches of the surface and only a pale, diffused glow reached down to me. Once I was within inches of a collision with a waterlogged tree root; another time I hit one hand against a mud-embedded poplar stick the beaver had not consumed during winter feeding. I cut the back of my hand on it, but I was encouraged because it told me this lodge had been in use during winter; it strengthened my opinion that this was the nursery.

I could not have been submerged more than thirty seconds or so when my questing hands found the lodge entrance. It was edged with sticks into which were wedged stones and pond debris; but it was not muddy, because the water washed the earth away each time any of it was deposited in the chute entrance. The hole was large enough for me to thrust my head, right arm, and shoulders into it. Immediately my face pressed into the slickness of mud and a second later the strong, fetid odor of the lodge's interior struck my nostrils. I had my eyes open. There was only blackness; I could breathe, but the air was musky and strong. I could not hear a sound. I stretched my arm and felt inside the lodge chamber and encountered nothing but wet mud on the compacted floor. I swept my arm back and forth, keeping my hand on the lodge floor, but my searching fingers did not encounter life. I was not sure how large the chamber was, but I knew I had not been able to reach across it because my fingers did not touch the mud-and-stick walls at any place other than around the immediate area of the entrance, and at last I gave up trying to feel and I remained still and listened intently.

I felt sure that if the kits were in the lodge I would hear them, particularly now that my arm had been feeling for them, they would be alarmed, and even if they made no vocal sounds, they could not help clustering together for mutual protection and I would hear their movements. But there was silence. A few seconds later I could stand it no longer. I was chilled to the very bones and I could not forget the leeches and I was telling myself that I was a fool and that it would be easy to get stuck in that beaver tunnel and end my life in a most unpleasant fashion. I pushed myself out and thrashed water with my legs and turned and shot up to the surface. On shore, I stood shivering and bedraggled and horrified by two leeches adhering to my body, one on my right foot, the other on my stomach, almost in my navel.

I don't know what it is about leeches that fill most people with horror and revulsion, but I am no exception to those feelings. I wanted to wrench the filthy things out of my flesh, but I knew enough to control the impulse, because pulling them out like that only leaves their sucking parts embedded in the skin and infection usually follows. Salt is the surest and best way to rid oneself of leeches. I had been so anxious about the kits that I had not stopped to bring some with me.

Shuddering as much in revulsion as with cold, I climbed naked into the canoe and paddled furiously back to the campsite, beached the boat, and sprang on shore almost in one motion, then ran to the tent and grabbed the salt. The leech on my belly was the largest, a sack of obscene, tough muscle about three inches long and three eighths of an inch wide, tapering at the ends, where the suckers are located. The filthy thing had fastened both its mouths to my flesh, so that it arched, dark and glistening, as it sucked my blood from both its ends; I doused it liberally with salt, holding my cupped hand against it to make sure the grains stuck to its wet body and feeling the creature's pulsing struggles as the calcium bit into it. I poured salt on the smaller leech. It was stuck to me by only one sucker mouth and soon it writhed free. The big one on my belly let go with one mouth and literally stood on end, waving and thrashing frantically, but retaining its grip. Suddenly it let go to fall and lie wriggling in the grass. Watery blood oozed out of the three puncture marks and I dabbed it off with a handkerchief and found some Mercurochrome to disinfect the tiny holes, but now that I had got rid of the unwelcome guests I did not feel the same degree of repugnance that had gripped me seconds earlier. In fact, I was curious about the amount of blood the two leeches had stolen from me, and after I toweled myself dry and dressed again, I scooped the still-thrashing creatures from the grass and put them on a rock; then I dissected them. The small one contained hardly more than a trace of blood; the large one had managed to get about a quarter of a teaspoonful. I left them there, not yet dead, sure they would now furnish food for some other form of wilderness life.

I was shivering, despite my clothes, so I sat in the sun, smoking my pipe and thinking about the beaver kits, feeling sorry for them because I was sure now that they either were dead or would soon die, for I was convinced that they had been driven to leave the lodge chamber by their great hunger. And that was the worst thing that they could possibly do. In the lodge, they would die more quickly from thirst; outside, if they were not picked off by some predator, they would linger, because the lake water would prevent dehydration.

Snapping turtles lurk in almost all lakes and marshes, some

of them reaching giant size, especially in relatively undisturbed country such as the one I was in; large pike—I had seen one almost three feet long during yesterday's tour of the lake—will also take a beaver kit; so will a hawk, or a mink, or an otter. One way or the other, the offspring of the beaver sow killed by the wolf would certainly die; of that I was sure. But I had to keep on looking. I launched the canoe again and started to paddle, to tour the lake quietly and keep my eyes open for unusual occurrences. There wasn't much hope, I felt, but I was impelled to continue the search.

The sun passed the nooning place. I had found nothing. I was hungry, tired, and, if truth be told, rather down in the mouth. I could not get the young beaver out of my mind. I didn't know how many there were, of course, but I was positive there were at least two, perhaps three. From the size of the mother's tracks at the place where she was killed, I judged her to be large and, therefore, old; and knowing that female beaver bear fewer young as age advances, I didn't think this one would have had a large number of kits, though there was little comfort in the surmise. Even if only one beaver kit was born to her, its pathetic fate was distressing to contemplate.

Eventually I gave up and returned to camp, where I made some coffee and opened a can of beans, and when the skimpy meal was finished, I went for a walk away from the lake because I was too restless to do anything constructive around the tent, but yet I was in need of action to take my mind away from the unknown beaver kits.

I walked toward the north, across a large, flat expanse of granite that harbored some gnarled poplars and a few stunted white pines and was covered for the most part by mosses and blueberry bushes. This would be a good place to come and gather berries in July, for not even the hungriest bear would be able to strip all the fruit from the numerous bushes.

Half an hour after crossing the rock plateau, which I named

Blueberry Flats, I was confronted by a steep ridge plentifully covered in pines across the flank of which were three well-defined game trails that stood out like footpaths through a park. I found many deer tracks and there was plenty of bear sign; then I found wolf tracks, big ones. I studied them and concluded that a large male habitually came this way; a male because of the size of the tracks, a single wolf because one pad was missing a toenail, or so it appeared when I bent to examine the pug marks carefully.

The front feet of adult timber wolves are bigger than the back feet, as is the case with all members of the dog family, so that it is an easy matter to pick out the hind and front tracks when these are left in soft ground or snow. Usually, the four claws on each foot show clearly in the spoor, but the animal that made the tracks that I was studying left only three claw marks wherever the right front paw touched the ground; the outside claw did not make any impression.

I decided to try to follow the wolf tracks along one of the game trails, the surface of which was muddy in places and showed the imprints of the animals that had used it recently, though I knew that the task I had set for myself would not be an easy one to accomplish.

There is much more to the tracking of wild animals than is suggested by the term, which implies that all that is necessary to do is to follow spoor until the quarry is discovered. Certainly, keen eyes are needed, but a tracker must *know* the habits of his quarry and he must be expert at reading other kinds of sign. It is easy enough to pick up tracks in mud, or in mushy snow, even those left by a soft-footed animal, but it is not easy to identify footprints left in sand or in powdery snow.

On grasslands, rocks, the thick duff that covers the forest floor, and in deep, tangled thickets, it is almost impossible to follow an animal's tracks and a tracker must be able to think like his quarry in order to guess the probable direction of travel and the possible objective of the journey. This is done by interpreting such factors as the time of day (or night), the condition of the country, and the kinds of animals that it is likely to shelter, as well as the directional characteristics of the trail that one is following. A wolf that is just traveling through an area, for instance, is more likely to trot along a more or less straight course without frequent stops and without many detours: its intention is to go from A to B as quickly and safely as possible, rather like the neighbor's dog that is seen leaving home and walking away without pausing to sniff or wet, obviously determined to gain some distant goal.

A hunting wolf that has not yet picked up a good scent is far more likely to follow his nose any which way, as he picks up odors. When its tracks are seen, they do not offer directional guides because they turn and twist, backtrack, and often disappear into tangled places where a human cannot follow.

Thus the mind of a tracker must compute hundreds of details while his eyes are continuously scanning the ground and his ears are alert for any change in the "beat" of the wilderness. Sometimes, a tracker senses and interprets evidence that hardly enters his conscious notice; on other occasions, if he really knows his quarry, he is able to predict the animal's movements almost as though he were gifted with extrasensory perception.

Is the quarry going to den after a hunt? Is the quarry fleeing a predator? Is a predator stalking prey, or is it hunting but has not yet struck a good scent? Compute wind direction, the voices of the birds, the shrill calls of the squirrels, the way a bush is moving a hundred yards ahead, the formation of the land and the nature of the plants that cover it: these are just a few of the many things that a good tracker must note and interpret.

Hunting animals instinctively seek those areas where shelter is available to them; they follow timbered ridges, travel through ravines and swales, pad softly over the duff in park-land forests, and like all wild animals, they employ caution as a matter of rule. For these reasons, the chances of a tracker ever coming up to his quarry by just following a trail are indeed small, unless the animal is sick or injured. Even the most careful woodsman is unable to walk silently enough to escape the keen ears of his quarry and when an animal be-comes aware that it is being followed it usually fears the worst.

At such times, the quarry may speed up and quickly lose the tracker, or it may swing away into a long detour; it may even go into hiding, lying immobile within the shelter of dead-fall or thicket.

Success in tracking, therefore, often depends on the tracker's ability to outguess his quarry, then to detour so as to come up with the animal at some expected place, but such success is only possible if the tracker is intimate with the habits of his quarry and knows the country through which he is traveling, or, failing this, at least knows enough about the wilderness to be able to interpret from trees and plants and land formations the condition that prevails some distance ahead.

That afternoon I put my nose to the trail and followed the wolf, and it quickly became evident that he was a careful and cautious creature; he checked everything. Chipmunk burrows were nosed and some had even been pawed a little; the deer tracks had received a great deal of attention and three times he had detoured likely hiding places and approached them from the opposite direction, which suggested that he was an optimist who had hoped to catch a snoozing whitetail un-awares. Then I came across the meager remnants of a ruffed grouse. The wolf had struck the bird behind a log, which sug-gested he may have hit a cock bird busy with his ritualistic drumming, when these woodsy fowl are more intent on at-tracting a hen bird or challenging a rival than they are on self-preservation. The kill was made the night before, or perhaps early that morning, for the blood adhering to some of the feathers was still red and two matted clumps were damp and stained my fingers. Certainly he had eaten every last scrap of meat, leaving only an untidy burst of feathers, a few blades of gore-spotted grass, and a couple of shreds of intestine.

I wondered about this hunter. He had come to within three quarters of a mile of my tent, maybe even closer for all I knew, and he had done a lot of walking and sniffing and checking and, at least up to that point on his route, had been rewarded only by one grouse, perhaps a pound or so of meat, a mere snack even for a smaller wolf. So the fellow was hungry and, unless I missed my guess, he was hunting for a family. He had probably mated last January or February with a young bitch, so that the two now formed the nucleus of a new pack. She would be caring for the pups in a carefully concealed den while the dog hunted for her and for himself and even for the still-nursing puppies, who would gnaw toothlessly on bits of meat or bone and thus get a taste of the food that destiny had reserved for them.

I walked on, keeping beside the game trail and looking for wolf tracks, and presently I saw the rotting stump of a giant pine. The body of the tree lay stretched on the ground, little more than a long mound of punky wood covered by moss and seedling pines and fungi and tunneled by ants and mice and beetles. The stump survived only because the enduring resin that had once flowed like blood through the "veins" of the tree was concentrated in the butt end, preserving the outside two or three inches of wood while the inside was pulpy and already nursing four three-inch-high seedlings. The wolf had devoted a great deal of attention to this stump and I soon realized that this was a scent station, one of those places selected by wolves for purposes of communication, a sort of wilderness post office to be sniffed, wetted, sniffed some more, and then, having gleaned some mysterious message or other and left a new sign for the next wolf to read, to be marked further by some quick scratchings in the dirt around the tree effected by a couple of careless kicks of the hind feet.

All right, I soliloquized, I, too, will leave my message. When I was done I turned back for camp, wondering what the wolf would make of my scent. I chuckled aloud. He would probably feel contempt because of the puny, watery substance that was as nothing compared to his rich, deep yellow, pungent discharge.

As I was homeward bound I felt a little silly because of what I had done, but there was purpose in it. I wanted the wolf to know my scent; I wanted him to know that I was prepared to share in his rituals as best I could. I did not, however, expect any major reactions, nor did these ever take place, and thus I am unable to confirm one writer's claims that the wolves resented his use of their scent station when he performed a like action.

The sun was beginning to set when I reached camp. It hung big and round and incandescent over the water, mirroring itself and casting a million lances of rose-red reflections. I stood at the water's edge and feasted on the scene, so fully taken with the splendid spectacle that I quite forgot about the beaver kits. In the center of the lake, some fish were jumping, largish ones, judging by the splashes, and I wondered if they could be trout. Whatever they were, they would be a welcome addition to my diet. A bittern called from the marsh and an early nighthawk sang as it swooped through the sky. Then I heard the piercing whistle of a red-shouldered hawk, the hunting call designed to make fearful and careless some small creature of the forest. The whistle was repeated, closer. I looked up and saw the sturdy buteo sweeping back and forth near the big lodge. It was circling, coming lower with each pass, and it seemed to be concentrating its attention on a section of shoreline where grew a profusion of arrowweed and a few catkins. In the center of this place was a large tree stump, its stark rootstocks upthrust like bony, dark fingers. The buteo circled again and swooped lower, passing directly over the stump and whistling shrilly and turning its head as it went by in order to get a good look at whatever had captured its keen-eyed attention. I went to the tent and got the field glasses and focused them on the stump. As I watched, the hawk swung in once more, very low this time, almost brushing the highest rootstocks. At first I could see only the sere wood and a few sprouting seeds that grew on it, then I saw it, a dark, still ball of fur. I could hardly believe my eyes; but, yes, I had found one of the beaver kits. And immediately I became frantic. The hawk!

It was even then turning for another pass, perhaps the fatal one, and already in my imagination I could see the raptor rise into air after striking the shivering little beaver, its great curved claws firmly embedded in the living morsel. I yelled, loudly. And I yelled again as I ran for the canoe and pushed it into the water and jumped into it and stroked hard toward the root that was about a hundred and fifty yards away. The hawk faltered in its dive as my yells distracted it, but as it overshot its mark, it quickly recovered and started a new approach. I yelled once more; then I spent a precious moment or two in banging the paddle against the canoe's hull. The booming sound had its effect. The hawk rose higher, circled wide and began to come back again. Now I was halfway to the stump. I banged against the hull again and once more the buteo turned away. Then I was close enough to deter the hawk and I knew I would reach the kit in time. If it was still alive. I could not be sure. It remained immobile, wedged in a fork of two roots, limp and bedraggled. But hawks seldom strike dead animals.

A minute or so later the canoe scraped against the stump and I found myself looking into a doleful, anguished baby face

out of which two coal-black, shoe-button eyes stared in appre-
hensive horror. I spoke gently, talking nonsense, mouthing
soft words in a reassuring tone as I reached slowly for the
cringing little bundle. My right hand was only about two
inches away from the kit; I stopped it in mid-air and I spoke to
the foundling. Carefully I lowered my hand; it touched the
matted fur, my fingers curled around the shriveled body; I
crooned my silly words as I tightened my grip just enough to
lift the kit. It made no protest, just stared at me with its lack-
luster eyes, and I could not decide whether it was trusting or
resigned to its fate.

A moment later the kit was pressed to my belly, to the soft
part of the diaphragm, where the heartbeat vibrates the
muscle, and my cupped hands warmed it and my voice was as
soothing as I could make it. The kit snuggled, definitely. I
stroked it very gently with one thumb, on its small head, between its ears, back and forth, easy, the while speaking my
nonsense, my whole being concentrated on telling that orphan
that it was safe now and that I would take care of it. The hawk
whistled as it left the area and I felt the little beaver cringe at
the sound. Young as it was, it knew, it could detect the urge to
kill; could it also detect the urge to protect?

I continued stroking the round head and pressing the sad
body against my stomach, so that I could feel it move each
time my heart beat, and the youngster responded and its
hungry lips began to suck at my shirt, small, pathetic nuzzlings
accompanied by little sobby noises and muted mumblings. It
was then that I realized that I must get the orphan to shore
and prepare some milk for it. I had brought a good quantity of
powdered skim milk, and out of habit occasioned by numerous rescues of helpless young animals, I had brought two eyedroppers, useful for dripping warm milk into hungry mouths.
Because I needed both hands free to paddle the canoe, I put
the kit into my shirt and buttoned it; then I paddled for home.

I was deliberately slow returning to the campsite with my newly found ward because I didn't want to disturb him any more than was necessary. I let the canoe drift after every third stroke and I released the paddle with my left hand so as to caress the young beaver, pressing him against the warmth of my body and hoping that contact with something living and gentle would give him the reassurance he so badly needed.

The kit didn't struggle, but he shivered, an almost imperceptible quaking that emphasized his state of shock and fear. Each time I put my hand over him the shaking lessened, but as soon as I returned to the paddle, I could feel the shivers against my diaphragm. I wanted to hurry, to race back to the campsite and give the orphan the care that he must quickly have if he was to survive; but I knew I must remain calm, for the little animal was very near to total nervous collapse and could not endure unbridled haste. I forced myself to paddle slowly and rhythmically, curbing my impatience as the distance to the rocky shoreline lessened like a filmed scene projected in slow motion.

I don't think it took more than about three minutes to complete the short trip, but my anxiety for the beaver was so great that the 180 seconds seemed to tick away like so many hours, and when the canoe at last became beached on the shelving rock, I felt my tensions rise to a point of almost maximum adrenalin, not a good thing under any circumstance, but particularly undesirable now. Perhaps others have shared such an experience; it's somewhat like a bad dream, like being chased and attempting to run, but not moving from the horror, so that panic rises and the heart beats loudly and the sweat starts and, mercifully, one wakes up. But this wasn't a dream and the kit's miserable condition was my goad; my memory of the scene where his mother had met her death was vivid reality inside my head.

Overanxious now, and fearful that at the last moment the

kit would die, I let emotion get the upper hand for a few moments; then I made myself calm by using an old trick I stumbled on years earlier: I began to think of beautiful things, of calm things, like flowers and quiet water and sunshine. It was an effort, but I managed to put my mind into a neutral and peaceful state that slowed my wild heart and allowed my caressing fingers to stroke the kit with affectionate reassurance.

Clasping him to me, I got out of the canoe and walked slowly to the tent, unzipped the flap with care so as not to make a sudden noise, and I went inside. Immediately I felt better, but I was still concerned. Wild things, especially young ones, are acutely sensitive to mood and are able to pick up "sense waves" from that aura which, like some intangible breeze, seems to be given off by all living creatures. This is a phenomenon of life that defies comprehension at this stage of human enlightenment, but it does, nevertheless, exist—of this I am sure.

Inside the tent, within the familiar surroundings of my own "den," I felt personally secure and much more confident, and I believe this became evident in my voice as I talked softly to the kit while I undid my shirt and reached inside it for his little balled body. He looked at me calmly enough when I brought him out and he seemed pathetically trustful as I held him and then lifted him in my cupped hands and brought him close to my face, breathing directly into his partly opened mouth and into his nostrils, wanting him to get my scent, to relate to me, to know that the creature in whose keeping he now was would care for him and comfort him. He smelled musky, and sour, and there was also an odor of mushroom about him; I noticed a small leech sticking to his right ear as I put out my tongue and licked his face and his nose and mouth, all over his head, tasting his rankness, yet feeling no revulsion. The kit responded. He mumbled very softly, and nuzzled at my mouth and tried to grasp at my lower lip, to suck. I drew him away gently and clasped him to me with one hand as I unzippered the sleeping bag, then I put him inside and covered him up, making a warm, dark nest for him. When I rose to go outside I kept talking and as I left the tent I silently willed him to live.

Four I got the fire alight quickly, put the water on, and mixed some skim milk into a stiff paste with a little cold water, ready to make up the formula when the pot came to a boil. I had to be careful with the proportions of the mixture because if I made it too strong, the kit might die from intestinal irritations, for cow's milk is generally too rich for the smaller mammals. Starved and dehydrated as he was, he would have to be fed little and often, until his strength returned and his tissues absorbed their normal amounts of moisture.

Testing the water with my finger and finding it warm, I

went to my "possible bag," as I call the old army packsack in which I keep my first-aid supplies and other emergency needs, found the eyedroppers, and put them into the pot of water after first removing the little rubber suction bulbs. The droppers hadn't been used for a while and a token boiling would not be amiss, though I do not take the same sterile precautions with my wards as humans do with their infants. I have found through experience that wild folk are far more resistant to infection than humans and, in fact, too much sterile protection can lead to the defeat of natural immunity factors, so that later, when the animal is free to follow life in its wild habitat, it is more likely to succumb to the attack of pathogenic organisms.

While the water was rising to the boil I got the milk paste and put two teaspoonfuls into one of three screw-lid jars that I carry for collecting field specimens, such as insects or flowers; it held twelve ounces of liquid, while each dropper held one eighth of an ounce. I intended to dilute the two spoonfuls of milk in ten ounces of water and feed the kit three droppers of this mixture at first. Then, depending on how he reacted in the morning, I would increase the strength of the formula and gradually regulate the amount of his feed until his intake became stable and spaced to three feeds a day, at morning, noon, and night.

When the formula was mixed and cool enough, I carried the jar and the droppers into the tent and set them down on a hand towel on the floor. The kit was mewling softly, but he stayed still under the covers, and I began to talk to him as I reached slowly inside the bag and curled my fingers around him. The mewling stopped, but I could feel his mouth searching for a teat among my fingers. With my free hand I unzippered the bag and lifted the cover off the kit; then I filled an eyedropper and coaxed the end of it into his mouth. He became excited the moment he tasted the fluid and in his haste to suck he moved his head and lost the end of the dropper, so that I had some trouble getting it back into his mouth. He could not, of course, relate the unyielding glass nozzle with his mother's soft breast, but after a moment or two more of trial and error, he got the idea and began to suck lustily.

Eyedroppers, unlike feeding bottles with rubber teats, will not yield to sucking and the trick in using them is to squeeze the rubber bulb with just enough pressure to allow a continuous dribble of formula to escape and reward the young animal for its sucking, which is what I did; but the eighth of an ounce of fluid soon disappeared in the kit's eager mouth and when the dropper was empty I had to remove it and reach for the second, full one. While I was doing this, the kit began to move about, searching for the food, and he set up a continuous wailing with surprising vigor. It was only a matter of seconds before I had the other dropper into his mouth, but in that time he kicked up a big row. I talked as I fed him, telling him he was being impatient and uttering other bits of nonsense, and soon the second dropper was empty.

Once more I removed it and turned to the jar and I took a little longer this time because I had to squeeze the rubber bulb and fill the empty dropper. Again the beaver child wailed and fussed and as I was lifting the dropper from the jar I scolded him gently. "Now, now! Just don't get into such a paddy," I admonished as I stuffed the nozzle into his waiting mouth. That sentence gave the orphan his name. He was quick to get into a paddy, so Paddy is what I called him from then on.

By the time I had finished giving him his first feed and had popped him back under the covers of my sleeping bag, the sun had vanished and evening was preparing for night. It was now time for my own meal. Opening a can of beans and pouring them into the frying pan, I added about a tablespoonful of molasses and some bacon fat left over from breakfast, and while this was heating, I made some pancakes, using a package of ready-mix. These were to be my dessert, laced with marmalade and washed down by coffee.

After my supper, I calculated that a full hour had passed since Paddy's first feed, so I warmed up his formula and repeated the earlier procedure with almost identical results. Paddy was well named! He complained noisily between droppers and he bounced around inside the sleeping bag when the second feed was over. But I was content; he showed by his actions that life still held the upper hand within his small carcass and he showed also that he had a mind of his own. Ignoring his sulky noises and his most pathetic little wails, I went outside and sat by the fire and I watched the night descend on the lake and on the forest.

I sat puffing my pipe, thinking about Paddy and his needs and feeling drowsy, already very much aware of the responsibilities that I had taken on when I rescued the little beaver. At that moment I would have liked nothing better than to go to bed after finishing my pipe, but instead I would have to stand vigil out here until his last feed at midnight.

A loon was hallooing and laughing on the water near to the campsite and its loud voice seemed to fill the tent with sound, waking me up, but I was in no mood for loons and I began to turn over with every intention of going back to sleep. Then I felt a weight on my stomach. I remembered Paddy! I moved my hands to find him perched on top of me, sucking avidly at the shirt that I wear in bed.

My right hand curled around him and he stopped sucking the shirt and turned to nuzzle my fingers; my left hand came into contact with something warm and wet and sticky. Paddy had moved his bowels on my stomach!

Although I wasn't unduly concerned—because that sort of thing happens often to anyone who raises young wild animals and allows them to share his bed—I *was* worried about the condition of Paddy's bowels; it seemed to me that he should not yet have had a need to void and that perhaps the milk mixture had been too strong and had caused an upset. When I removed the covers and juggled Paddy with one hand while I inspected his waste, I relaxed. It was messy and odorous, but quite normal and, I was thankful to note, not very plentiful.

Outside the loon was still calling, greeting the slow arrival of daylight. There was no sun yet, but the gray light of pre-sun was strong enough to make things visible inside the tent, filtering in through the plastic back window and through the windows in the doorway flaps. I looked at Paddy, holding him up in one hand while I did my best to keep his tacky mess away from my body with the fingers of the other. Paddy looked back at me and mewled almost like a kitten. Then he began to mumble and mutter in his funny way, stopped for a moment to have a tentative suck at my thumb, and renewed his mewling when he found no milk. He seemed alert and strong and quite obviously very hungry and I was pleased to note that he had already accepted me fully and showed no trace of fear or nervousness.

I spoke to him as I got up, and when I was on my feet I put him down on the sleeping bag while I found a clean pair of shorts and another shirt. Paddy scurried around, making his impatient noises, and I left him alone as I unzippered the tent flap and, closing it again behind me, staggered away to the water's edge to have a quick wash and change into my clean attire.

The eastern sky was turning pink and held the promise of another fine, warm day, but I shivered with cold as I hurried through my hasty wash, toweled myself dry, and climbed quickly into my clothes before lighting a good crackling fire. The loon had stopped calling. I must have disturbed it when I unzippered the tent, but other birds were already beginning their morning songs and a few mosquitoes came to inspect my bare legs, looking for a good place into which to plant their tiny blood siphons. I turned away from the fire and re-entered the tent, talking to Paddy as I reached for my pants and put them on. When I sat on the sleeping bag to put on my socks and boots, Paddy came scampering to me and immediately climbed into my lap and began to look for his breakfast, sniffing at the places where he had been held yesterday and becoming frantic as his nostrils detected a few faint traces of milk scent from the dribbles that had escaped the droppers to fall on my pants.

Young though he was, the little beaver appeared to possess all his faculties, and I was amazed at his obvious ability to pick up his own scent and the odor of yesterday's diluted milk. But he had to wait for his breakfast, for I had not yet prepared it. I lifted him gently off my lap and put him on the sleeping bag and I had to get up quickly to stop him from climbing right back up again. I told him to be patient, a piece of advice that he completely ignored, and I went outside to put some water to boil. In a few minutes I had his formula ready, stronger this time by the addition of two teaspoonfuls of powdered milk to last night's dilution, and I set the pan in shallow water to cool.

Now it was time to make some coffee and I filled the pot and put it on to boil. Suddenly Paddy's mewling was a lot closer. I turned around and saw him waddling out of the tent, his mouth open as he called hungrily. I had forgotten to close the tent flap.

He was about two feet from the tent by the time I stooped and picked him up and he had been heading away from me and the fire, too young yet to sense direction, but quite able to get about on his own and seemingly none the worse for his time of starvation. I held him with my left hand against the curve of my neck, pressing him close so that he could feel the pulsing of my carotid artery, but the rhythm of my blood failed to pacify him now that he recognized me as the source of his food and his security and he mewled continuously as he searched for a teat against my neck, slobbering a little. I held him gently and walked to the pan of milk; it was still too hot. As I waited beside the water for the formula to cool, I was once more intrigued by the apparent ease with which wild animals sense the conditions of their environment. Paddy, like so many other young wildlings that I had raised, showed a keen, opportunistic ability to assess his needs and comforts and an almost incredible capacity to recognize the absence of personal threat. Despite the traumas that he had so recently undergone, and the physical deprivations that could so easily have caused his death, he had quickly recognized the safety that I offered and he was already giving me his full trust.

Yesterday's fears had seemingly vanished and his immediate concerns centered exclusively on the demands of his empty stomach, a sure clue to his state of mind, for animals gripped by alarm instantly lose their appetite.

Paddy's new-found confidence in me, and his recognition of my scent—and no doubt his own, which lingered on my clothes—allowed him to be at ease, so that he alternated between nuzzling my neck and rubbing himself against me as he let me fondle him. I tried the milk once more. Now it was ready and I went to the tent, got the droppers, and returned to the fireside, having decided that I would feed him in the open this morning.

The sun had tipped the trees by now, so I positioned myself toward the west, facing the big marsh, because Paddy's eyes must still be weak and sunlight might cause him discomfort. Soon he was sucking with his usual vigor, pawing at me, now and then blowing milky bubbles out of his nose, about a pound of silky-pelted life that already had altered the tenor of my task in this place, for he personified the animals I had come to study and he had become my direct link with them. He made very personal my interest in this place.

That morning Paddy consumed a full two ounces of the stronger mixture. It doesn't sound like a lot, two ounces, but when it was administered one eyedropper at a time, each of which gave him only one eighth of an ounce, simple mathematics shows that he sucked his way through sixteen droppers of formula. At the end of it, I longed for my kit of supplies that I had accumulated for the purpose of rearing wild folk. I had an assortment of feeding bottles with different-sized nipples that ranged from mouse size to moose size. But I had left it behind, not expecting to become a foster parent on this expedition.

As I held Paddy, who after his feed turned over on his back and went to sleep in my lap, all four legs thrust upward in untidy postures, his paddle tail draped over one of my knees, I busied myself thinking about how I could devise another way of feeding him during the next few days. It was still too early in his life to expect him to suck up formula from a plate. I did not have the right tools with me with which to fashion a suitable feeding bottle out of wood and I had nothing that would lend itself for use as a nipple. By evening, I felt sure, he would be strong enough to demand at least four ounces of milk, which meant thirty-two droppers! It would be a slow and tedious performance and I was sure that Paddy would become dreadfully impatient before he had taken his fill. But there seemed to be no help for it just then.

The sun was well up in the sky now. The loon that had called earlier appeared in Water Lily Bay, dived, reappeared, and dived again, not to surface within my range of vision. A few flies and mosquitoes quested about my head; the birds were competing with each other to voice their territorial and mating calls. Then the red-shouldered hawk came sailing in.

The raptor was flying high, using the thermals to keep itself gliding on stiff pinions as it circled the lakeshore, every now and then emitting its shrill war whoop. It dropped lower as I watched and it came closer to my side of the lake. When it was almost directly above me, the big buteo uttered its shrill cry and swept past, aiming toward Blueberry Ridge. The effect of its call on Paddy was galvanic. The little beaver had not stirred so much as a fine whisker when the hawk had called from across the lake, but when it shrieked so close to us, Paddy bunched his small body, turned himself right side up, and attempted to burrow down between my legs; I covered him with both my hands, pressing him to me and excluding the light from his eyes, talking to him softly. He trembled at first, perhaps for half a minute, but the shaking was not as severe as it had been yesterday and his fright soon passed.

Nevertheless, I realized that he was still much too young to be exposed to the many fearful sounds of the daytime wilderness. Nature had painstakingly imprinted an undetermined number of warnings on his small brain, mysteriously managing to program the kit so that he would quickly seek safety when any of his built-in alarms were triggered, but under normal circumstances Paddy would still be inside his darkened lodge for at least another two weeks, as secure in the oval nest as he had been in his mother's womb, developing himself physically by feeding and mentally by accepting his safety without question and thus allowing his mind the time that it needed to grasp and interpret the fundamental concepts of life without being interrupted by repeated alarms.

Because of these things, and because of his reaction to the hawk's call, I decided to build him a small "lodge" out of poplar wood, a miniature den in which he could spend his growing time without fear of outside disturbances; it would also be a place where I could leave him, inside the tent, when I left the campsite on field trips, which I was going to have to do frequently if I was to fulfill the purpose of my journey.

Five My interest in beaver began soon after I arrived in Canada, some ten years before my journey to Old Alec's Lake. It started one day in early April four months after I had taken up a homestead in the Lake of the Woods area of Ontario, a region so close to the Minnesota border that a portion of the lake is in American territory. At the time, I was a greenhorn, a stranger to the land and its animals.

I left my log home to go walking along a twisting game trail that snaked through an area of mixed woods and eventually led me to the first beaver pond that I had ever seen. An exceptionally cold winter, heavy snowfalls, and a late, but sudden spring had produced some serious flooding in my area and the pond that I found was swollen with meltwater. The full force of the current was pressing hard against the beaver dam, a structure of mud, stones, sticks, and captured pond debris that was about twenty feet long, slightly bowed at its center, and solid-looking until I noticed that the flood had made a hole at one end of the structure, near my shoreline, through which the frothing water tumbled. As I stood there, another piece of the dam let go with a loud tearing sound to fall with a muddy splash into the fast water below the dam. I decided to stay and watch for a while, sitting myself close to the shoreline on an old poplar cut down by beaver.

At first all was quiet, but presently some of the birds that had been disturbed by my arrival began to sing and a few spring frogs set up a feeble chorus. I was watching the dam, expecting that it would soon crumble entirely under the battering of the water, when a beaver surfaced only about three feet from the break. I remained still.

The beaver swam to the dam, climbed halfway out of the water, then stood upright, as though to better inspect the damage. In a moment it dropped onto all fours, moved closer to the breach, leaned forward, and grabbed with its teeth a loose stick that was about to go over the side. The old, peeled limb protruded about two feet in front of the beaver's mouth and reached back some four feet behind the animal's back.

Quite slowly, the beaver slipped into the water, swam to the far side of the break, and just as I was sure that it was going to be swept downstream, swung its body and rammed the stick hard into the wall of the dam. Now it swam away, fighting the current, submerged, rose to the surface close to the far shore, and waddled inland; to collect more sticks, I rightly supposed. Soon another beaver showed up, this one swimming into view from behind a small island and towing a freshly cut alder branch. The newcomer pretty much repeated the first beaver's actions, and once its branch was tamped securely across the break, it followed its companion to the shore.

I watched while both animals busied themselves ferrying fresh sticks to the break, all the time wondering if they would be able to stem the escaping water. Little did I know in those days! Within half an hour, the flood had slowed to a trickle; the gap was well sealed with a crisscross of branches. Now the beaver began diving for mud, reappearing beside the dam with a dollop that was clutched by the forepaws and pressed against the chest, each animal coming out of the water on its hind legs, using its broad tail as a balance. With mud, stones, and pond debris they completely repaired the flood damage and after they had gone I walked along the edge of the dam and tried to remove one of the newly placed sticks; I could not budge it.

I did not, of course, realize how lucky I was to be able to witness beaver working to repair their dam during my first contact with the animal, but I was so interested in what I had seen that I determined then and there to make a study of the big rodents. That was in 1955, less than a year after I had walked down the gangway of an immigrant ship in Quebec City to claim my few possessions from a common pile on the quayside, before boarding the train that was to deposit me in Toronto, Ontario's capital city. There I spent the summer and autumn working as a journalist.

Bored and dissatisfied with the small pocket of Canada that, after England's London, offered me little excitement, I spent some restless weeks, then quit my job in November and headed north in an aging car that I had recently bought. Soon I was driving through deep snow and intense cold and I began to feel alive once more. My goal was Fort Frances, in the Rainy River district of Ontario, an area selected on advice from government officials. There, I was told, I could still find land on which to homestead. The officials were right. One week after my departure from Toronto, I was the owner of two hundred acres of land and a log cabin that had been built from hand-hewn logs in 1909. It was December 2; the temperature hovered at the 30-below-zero mark in an area of wilderness in which I had felt instantly at home.

The weeks that followed were full of newness and satisfaction, spiced by hardship that served to toughen the fibers of mind and body. In a surprisingly short time I felt healthier and happier than I had ever felt before and I derived great pleasure from the challenges that each day brought to test me.

The homestead was located on the very edge of the great boreal forest that spans the northern part of the American continent and stretches to timberline: spruce, jack pine, and tamarack dominated the scene, but deciduous trees such as aspen and birch grew in small stands in some places or mixed in others with the evergreens. Animal tracks were in plentiful evidence wherever I walked, some freshly printed in the snow, others older, marking the accustomed pathways of the forest folk: deer and wolf, snowshoe and hare and lynx, fox and mouse, marten and squirrel, and many more.

I was so intrigued with my new life that I was actually surprised to wake up one morning and discover that the snow had started to melt during the night. The date was April 6. By that afternoon an unusually early heat wave caused the snows to spread water all over the land, flooding the gravel road that ran past my homestead and filling the primitive ditches on either side of it with brown, noisy runoff. I looked at the thermometer: it registered 78 degrees.

The heat wave continued for two days before seasonal weather returned, the temperature adjusting itself to a daytime high of 45 or 50 degrees and falling to near freezing at night. The flood slowed, but the snow continued to melt and by the end of the week the land revealed itself to me for the first time.

It was then that I went for the walk and encountered the beaver.

The next day I drove to Fort Frances to buy needed supplies and tools, but after chatting with a helpful bank teller, I changed my mind and decided to shop in International Falls, Minnesota. The American town was larger than its Canadian neighbor and offered better shopping at lower prices, despite customs duty. A bridge over the Rainy River connects the two towns, dividing each city by only five minutes of driving time.

In the American town I parked the car and began to look around, window gazing while I made a mental list of the goods that I needed. Presently I found a large hardware store and I went inside and did much of my shopping, and it was there, while I stood looking with idle curiosity at a variety of animal traps that hung from brackets against one wall, that I met Old Alec.

"Them traps is no good. The springs yust don't last mor'n two seasons," I heard a heavily accented voice say at my back.

I turned. He stood a foot from me, a tall man with long arms and large, rawboned hands. Snow-white stubble bristled from his face; the thin, yellowish-white hair on his head would not be contained by the green baseball cap he was wearing. I took in at a glance the old man's heavy red-and-black-checked parka, patched mackinaw pants, and boots with rubber feet and leather uppers. I looked again at the seamed face and I liked what I saw in it.

"What's the matter with the springs?" I asked.

That began our friendship. He told me about traps, pointed out some of the defects in the ones we were discussing, and accompanied me when I suggested a cup of coffee in a nearby café, where we stayed until after lunch, drinking coffee at first, eating a meal later, and talking all the time, mostly because I asked him innumerable questions, to which he gave interminable answers. Afterward I drove him home. He had walked the eight miles into town and intended to walk back again, as was his habit.

When we reached his small frame house, Old Alec insisted that I stay for supper. I agreed reluctantly; I found the man interesting, even fascinating, but he was personally scruffy and the inside of his home was slovenly. The place reeked of stale food and other odors that I did not particularly want to identify, but which I was forced to do when he removed his parka. I am not a fussy man, yet I confess to an inherent distaste for dirt and, let it be said, that old man was most dirty!

I sat in a wooden chair while my host fished out a bottle of aquavit and two dirty mugs, into each of which he poured a stiff drink, handing me one and raising the other to his mouth. Then, silently, he bustled about a cast-iron cookstove and did mysterious things with the contents of a huge soot-blackened pot that had been sitting at the back of the range when we entered. Half an hour later—during which time we had exchanged but little conversation—he set two tin plates on the table, one fork and one spoon for each of us, and a large platter of bread that he had himself baked. The utensils were greasy and the bread was stale, but I hardly had time to worry about these things before the steaming pot was dumped unceremoniously on the table and I was told to "yust help yourself."

The meal consisted of a thick stew in which floated hunks of some kind of meat and pieces of carrot and potato. It was palatable and I was hungry and ate my fill, trying not to be squeamish. When I was done, Old Alec asked: "You lek?"

Yes, I liked, I told him; then, to make conversation, I asked him what kind of meat I had eaten, immediately wishing I had not inquired when he told me that it came from some muskrat that he had trapped "last week" from a marsh area behind his cottage. I had never before sampled muskrat and, in truth, I had but the vaguest idea of what the whole animal looked like when it was alive and *fresh*.

As I was mentally digesting the information and physically trying to do the same with the food, Old Alec reached for a big enameled coffeepot that like the stewpot seemed to have a permanent place at the back of the stove. I noticed that he did not throw out the old grounds, but simply grabbed a handful of fresh coffee and chucked it into the pot, which he then put on a front ring after first removing the center plate; now he came and joined me at the table, the half-empty bottle of aquavit clutched in one great paw.

By this time, having been silently severe with myself, I had accepted the muskrat meat mentally as well as physically, the main point being that I had quite enjoyed the meal, but I was wise enough not to ask any more questions about the iron pot because I was fairly sure—and I was to prove myself right during future visits—that it simply sat back and collected whatever Old Alec decided to throw into it, so that the nature of its contents changed daily but the stew owed its origins to antiquity. I suppose the coffeepot got emptied when the old grounds piled up to a point where it was difficult to put fresh coffee into the container, but that's only a guess, because I never saw the old man pitch out the grounds.

Over bad coffee and good aquavit, we talked and my interest in the man and in what he had to tell me about the country and its animals conquered the scruples that his lack of cleanliness inspired, so that by eight o'clock that night, when it was time for me to drive the long distance back to my homestead, I had learned more about the country in which I had bought my property than I could have done during a full year of residency.

Some weeks later I again visited Old Alec at home and was once more faced with muskrat stew, battery-acid coffee, and aquavit, but, as before, I benefited from my association with the old man; during this visit he instructed me in the ways of beaver and in the art of trapping and he told me how I should go about applying for a trapping license. His rough-and-ready instruction, begun that night and continued at varying intervals over the next six months, was to be invaluable to me.

On several occasions I picked him up in Minnesota and drove him to my Ontario homestead, where he would stay for several days, during which we would tramp over the country and he would show me things that I would have overlooked had I been on my own. Our friendship grew and I learned a lot about Old Alec. The man was lonely because he had a knack of antagonizing most people almost instantly; he was quick to anger, stubbornly opinionated, and quite uncaring about the feelings of others. Yet we two got along and we never had a single argument, even though I like to think that we were diametrical opposites in temperament and thus should have quickly had a falling out.

One day in early fall, after I had obtained my trapping license, I visited Old Alec at home and we began to talk about beaver pelts, particularly about their value on the market. Provided that the fur was prime, the bigger the blanket, the better the price, the old man said, and he went on to tell me that adult beaver would not infrequently weigh 100 pounds and that weights of 80 and 90 pounds were fairly usual in the area around my homestead.

Later, after I had read a great deal about beaver, I learned that such weights are not considered usual and that biologists believe that the average weight of mature animals varies between 40 and 50 pounds, though most concede that some individuals are heavier. The record, for a beaver trapped in Wisconsin, is 110 pounds, while many weigh 65 and 70 pounds. On my own trapline, the largest beaver that I caught weighed 73 pounds and the smallest 44.

At any rate, that autumn evening I left Old Alec's home

primed with last-minute tips on trapping that I was soon to put to effective use, for which I shall always be grateful to the man. By the time that the trapping season opened that year I was nearly broke, but the absence of ready cash hardly mattered in a country that furnished abundant meat and fuel; my taxes were twelve dollars a year, paid directly to the Ontario government because my property was located in an unorganized region; I had no electric bills to pay, no telephone charges, no rent, and my rude home was well stocked with staples such as potatoes, dried beans, rice, dried fruits, flour, powdered milk, sugar, tea, coffee, and cocoa. For the first time in my life I was able to face the future with confidence despite a nearly empty wallet.

At first I took snowshoe hares and ruffed grouse for the table and on the first day of the deer season I brought down a fat buck that dressed out at about 110 pounds, winter meat that I stored in the woodshed, where it froze overnight, for the temperature was never far from zero by then. Later I ate beaver meat as well and found it most palatable once I learned to get rid of the strong taste of fat by marinating it overnight in whatever spicy concoction I had available. At this time, too I dissected the carcasses, learning much about the beaver's anatomy, dietary habits, digestive peculiarities, and the musk and oil glands.

In those days, twenty dollars was a good price to get for a beaver blanket that had been properly fleshed and stretched into its traditional oval shape; it was money well earned, as those who have followed a northern trapline will readily agree.

My line was approximately twenty miles long and contained a number of large ponds and two small lakes, from all of which I took beaver and muskrat, though the latter fetched, at best, only twenty-five or thirty cents and represented considerable investment in time and effort for a very few dollars earned. Perhaps if I had been more expert at setting traps and better able to skin and flesh my catches, I might have continued trapping for a longer period; as it turned out, my novice inefficiency slowed down my pursuit of fur but granted me better opportunities to encourage my growing interest in field studies. By the end of the second winter I had begun to write about some of my findings, getting in this way additional income, and, meager though the free-lance checks were, they coaxed me back to the typewriter on a regular basis, intruding on my trapping activities and increasing my desire to learn more about the wilderness and its animals. When spring came that year I pulled all my traps and put them away for good, devoting myself exclusively to the study of nature.

In May I walked to a beaver pond that I knew of which was located about four miles from my cabin and was a place frequented by many species of ducks as well as the home of a large family of beaver. I intended to spend the day there, loafing a little, making notes, and beginning to plan an article on wildfowl that I had been commissioned to do by an English periodical. Sitting on a log on a slight rise of land that allowed me a good view of the water, I spent the first two hours watching a number of ducks and a small flock of Canada geese. It was while I was engrossed with these birds that I spotted a beaver swimming toward my shore from the far side of the pond.

When the animal got close, it began to circle as it checked for enemies; then, satisfied, it paddled ashore and walked directly to a flat, bare rock that was near the water's edge, which was about fifty yards from where I was sitting. I focused the glasses on it, bringing the animal so close visually that I felt as though I could lean forward and touch it. As I observed, the beaver appeared to have a bowel movement. My first thought was that the animal was suffering from diarrhea. A light-colored, porridge-like substance emerged from its anus and was deposited in a mound on the rock, and the beaver carefully kept its tail raised, away from the substance. When it was done, the animal turned around and began to eat what it had defecated seconds before.

I watched until it had finished every last scrap of its strange bowel movement. I was still watching in surprise when the animal started to groom its fur carefully, sitting there in the sunshine and methodically combing and currying, now and then dipping down between its legs with its front paws to reach its oil glands, which discharge their greasy fluid into the cloaca.

After each "handful" of oil—in fact, just a small amount—the beaver redistributed it over its fur, thus waterproofing its coat and causing it to shine like burnished copper under the strong sunshine. This kind of behavior I had seen before and I knew that the animal was grooming itself aided by a special combing claw, which is a split, pincer-like nail located on the second toe of each hind foot and which, according to some observers, but not confirmed by me, is also used as a toothpick, allowing the beaver to rid itself of wood particles wedged between its teeth.

Use of the combing claw necessitates the raising of one back leg and the animal often sits on its own paddle tail, as the one I was watching that morning was doing, picking up first one foot, combing one side of its body and as far around the chest and belly as it can reach, and then picking up the other foot and repeating the process, working slowly, now and then pausing at some specially itchy place and having a good, lethargic scratch.

As I watched the beaver engaging in its methodical toilet, I kept wondering about its apparently strange behavior. Why would the animal eat its own wastes? And why did these wastes look so different from any beaver scats that I had ever seen? Often I had watched a beaver defecate, an action that the animal performs mostly in the water, but which at times it does on the edge of its pond—but never inside its lodge, which is kept scrupulously clean; such scats were quite different from the light, porridgy material of this morning (normal beaver waste is compacted into various shapes and usually quite dark, often black in color).

Pondering over the strange behavior, it suddenly occurred to me that the material the beaver had reingested was similar to pulpwood, vats of which I had once examined in a paper mill at Fort Frances. Then I recalled the many times that I had looked at the stomach and bowels of dead beaver and had noted the extra-large appendix of these animals, which had almost always contained a quantity of woody, pulpy material. I had examined this carefully and had concluded it was, indeed, composed of woody fiber mixed with digestive juices, but I had been unable to account for its presence in the appendix. At the same time, some of the real wastes of the animals were often still lodged in the large bowel.

Now I began to put two and two together and I searched my memory for some of the biological information I had assimilated so slowly during the course of my education. I remembered the special digestive problem posed by cellulose, a substance that most mammals are unable to break down into usable nourishment.

Cattle solve this problem by having a divided stomach and by ruminating their food (chewing the cud). In this way, the cellulose-rich food goes through four different compartments before passing into the intestine.

Reasoning from what I had seen, I came up with a theory that I was later able to confirm. Unlike cattle, or other cud chewers, the beaver has only one stomach, but because it feeds exclusively on vegetable matter, the animal has had to develop a way of extracting nourishment from the cellulose-heavy food that it eats.

During a time now lost in the ages of prehistory, ancestral beaver evolved some unique methods of digesting their food. They developed a special gland that produces digestive enzymes to help in the breakdown of cellulose and they developed an extra-large appendix that acts as a pouch in which the vegetable fibers are stored partly digested. When the appendix is full, its contents are ejected and eventually excreted, to be re-eaten and then digested again and converted into nourishment. The wastes resulting from this second eating come out dry and hard and are excreted normally.

After I had arrived at what I felt was the correct theory, I wondered (and I still do) if *Homo sapiens* might have had a similar digestive process, or, if not *Homo sapiens*, at least his remote ancestor. This could, after all, explain the hitherto but poorly explained presence of our own appendix, which has now become—it appears—not only useless but downright dangerous at those times when food particles become blocked in it, decompose, and cause an infection that results in appendicitis.

As I watched the beaver complete its toilet and then sit quietly hunched up, enjoying the sunshine, I noticed that its mouth was working rhythmically. It was sharpening its huge lower incisor teeth by rubbing them against the outside surface of its upper incisors. This is a fairly usual practice in all rodents, though it does not fully account for the very fine cutting edge that these animals maintain on their teeth.

The beaver's very long incisors, like those of all rodents, are always growing to compensate for wear; nature has ingeniously fashioned them so that they are largely self-sharpening by covering the front surfaces with hard enamel. But the back surfaces are covered with a softer, pulpier material that wears down and creates a bevel edge, somewhat like that of a wood chisel, which is exceptionally sharp. Now and then a beaver may chip its front enamel, or it may gouge a piece out of the back surface, and at these times it chomps its jaws, working the lower, longer incisors, which do most of the cutting, over the upper, shorter teeth, which, being fixed in the unmoving upper jaw, are used mostly for holding on and for wrenching out wedges of wood when the beaver is cutting down a tree.

The animal I was observing reminded me of the first time I had actually seen a beaver chopping down a good-sized aspen, in an area near the pond where I had seen my first beaver repairing their dam. The animal had left the water and waddled up to the tree, which was about ten inches thick at the butt, stood up on its hind legs, balancing itself with its flat tail, and, after selecting a spot at a convenient height, began to gnaw away at the wood. I used field glasses to observe its actions and I noted how it anchored its jaws to the tree with the upper incisors and how it systematically worked its lower jaw to chip away a smallish V in the trunk. When this was done to its satisfaction, the beaver moved its hold to a place about four inches higher up the tree and repeated the process until it had cut another notch almost identical to the lower one; then it grasped the piece of wood in between the notches and, heaving back, gave a wrench with its powerful neck and shoulders and ripped out the chunk of wood. Afterward it began all over again in the same place, cutting another two notches, but closer together this time, and wrenching out the intervening wood. Slowly it moved around the tree trunk, chewing and notching and wrenching, until it had circled the tree more or less evenly, so that some two or three inches of wedge-shaped wood had been pulled off the poplar. It kept repeating the process, cutting smaller and smaller notches, until about twenty minutes later the trunk had developed the characteristic shape, like two pencils placed point to point, and at last the tree began to topple slowly to the ground.

As soon as the beaver saw that the tree was falling, it began to run and it was already on its way back to the pond when the tree landed with a resounding crash. The woodcutter entered the water and began to swim around, first in circles, then up and down close to the shore, its actions so obvious that even during that early stage of my knowledge I could appreciate that the crash might well attract predators to the scene if these had learned by observation the meaning of the noise.

Six On the morning after his rescue, Paddy slept peacefully in my bed while I worked for two hours to build his lodge. With ax and saw I cut and shaped a number of two-inch poplar saplings, which I fastened together with stovepipe wire, a double roll of which I always carry when I'm traveling through the bush. The structure was two feet square at the base, built like a tepee, with a floor of logs, over which I plastered a quantity of stiff mud, over which in turn I spread dry grasses and ferns. I built the log cage in two sections, top and bottom, so I could lift off the upper part when putting Paddy inside or taking him out and so that his bedding could be changed and his nest cleaned. For security, I cut the center log of the floor longer than its companions, and its ends could be wired tight to the upper structure, in this way making sure that Paddy stayed in his new home and, conversely, preventing anything else from getting at him while I was not around. The little lodge was three feet high and weighed about forty pounds.

When the whole thing was completed to my satisfaction, I got some fresh mud; using a flat rock as a mortarboard, I mixed the mud with a good supply of dry grass, then I plastered all the chinks between the logs, leaving only an air space at the top. When I had finished, the inside chamber was almost as dark as a real lodge and the whole thing looked, to my eyes, most "beaver-like." Paddy evidently thought so, too. When I lifted the top and put him inside, then gently lowered the superstructure, he mewled halfheartedly for a moment or two, then stopped. I bent close to the lodge and listened. I heard him rooting around among the bedding materials and presently there was complete silence. Paddy, I was sure, had gone to sleep. I waited inside the tent for a full five minutes, but he remained quiet, so I got my field glasses and left.

I was tired after last night's vigil and this morning's early start, and although I wanted to paddle out and cut a pathway through the marsh to make it easier to take the canoe in and out of Old Alec's Lake, my lethargy overcame my desire. Instead I climbed to the top of the rock from the base of which issued the spring, carrying my glasses, notebook, and a pen. I wanted to make a survey of the lake and to draw a proper map of it upon which I would trace distinctive landmarks. The rock, which I now christened Spring Rock, was almost thirty feet above my campsite at its highest point; it would offer a good survey post. The front of it was sheered almost plumb, but it sloped gradually to ground level at the back, which faced almost due east. When I reached the top, I found a level little plateau that was carpeted with moss and sprinkled with a few spruce and pine seedlings and a number of ferns and wildflowers. A loose boulder offered a good seat once I rolled it to the edge of the "cliff" that overlooked the lake and my campsite. It was an excellent vantage point.

I began by scanning the entire lake with my field glasses, starting in the east bay of the lake and moving very slowly along its shore. Within moments I found something I didn't know existed: a fairly wide creek. I looked at Old Alec's brown-paper map, wondering if I had failed to notice it, but either the creek formed after Old Alec left or he had forgotten about it, the latter being the more likely supposition, because the lake seemed to be too large and too deep to owe its origins purely to surface runoff combined with beaver husbandry. The creek feeding into the lake made sense. I marked it on my own map, naming it East Creek.

Where East Creek discharged into its own bay, there was a shallow area in which arrowweed grew in some profusion and I focused the glasses on the water and weeds at this place, giving it a good scrutiny more out of sheer curiosity than for any other reason. I was glad I did when the surface bubbled briefly as a small school of silver minnows jumped out of the water and splashed down again a few inches away from where they had emerged. I kept this piece of water under close watch, sure that bigger fish were even then feeding on the minnows, and it wasn't long before I noticed the characteristic yellow of several good-sized perch as they torpedoed through the shallows. I moved the glasses over the area and saw numbers of other fish, now and then confirming their identity when they turned on their sides close to the surface. There was a lot of perch in that bay. I put the glasses down and marked a name on my map: Perch Bay. And when I was done I decided to go fishing before supper that evening and see if I could hook one or two.

I continued scanning the shoreline of Perch Bay, swinging

slowly southward as I followed it and noting how the granite rock climbed gradually to a fairly large, flat area which was sufficiently distinct to warrant mapping. South Flats, I wrote, thinking as I did so that the mere naming of these landmarks gave me a deeper sense of relationship with the country. Soon I came to the point of land that jutted out almost opposite to my campsite, separating Perch Bay from Water Lily Bay. A few yards in front of this point was the small island where stood the large beaver lodge and where, I felt sure, Paddy had been born. I named his birthplace Paddy's Island and the finger of rock I named Paddy's Point, for it was just off this point that he had climbed onto the old root and huddled fearfully on top of it until I rescued him.

I passed over Paddy's Island and scrutinized Water Lily Bay, noting the profusion of yellow and white lilies whose blooms, though not yet fully formed, splashed small lines of color in the shallows. Not quite in the center of this bay was another rocky island only just larger than Paddy's. It was in this area where the bass had been jumping, so I christened it Bass Island—prophetically, as it turned out, for later on I found a deep hole by the north face of the island that was always good for a fat smallmouth if I was patient enough to tease the latest occupant with a small golden spoon. Characteristically, as soon as I caught the latest fish to stake claim to the deep hole, a new one moved in the next day, a habit that I exploited whenever I felt like fresh bass for supper.

Directly opposite Alec's Point, which was the name I had bestowed on the point where the old man had built his cabin and where I had fixed my base, and bearing almost due south of it, the shoreline bulged into a blunt "point" that just managed to separate Water Lily Bay from the largest bay (the third leaf of the clover shape), where lay the marsh. On this bulge of shore the beaver had built a lodge, not as large as the one on Paddy's Island, but of respectable proportions, nevertheless. I marked the position of the lodge on my map and also decorated the area with the little three-pronged symbols that designate marshland, but I had hardly refocused the glasses when I saw another lodge, a smaller one, about a quarter of a mile behind the first, and then I spotted a third, which was located so that it formed the peak of a broad-based triangle. This was now big marsh country that was flanked by two narrow rock ridges, north and south, which were about one mile apart. Swinging the glasses around, I saw that the water had fallen considerably since I came through from the marsh two days earlier and that, as I had suspected, there was more than one dam controlling the lake level. Due west of where I sat, two rock islets now protruded from the water; they had been completely covered when I paddled through that area on my way into the lake. Between the northern shoreline of the lake at this place and the first of the islets, there was one dam, which I called North Dam; it was about 200 yards long. On the south side of the rock, a smaller dam about 100 yards long closed the gap between the islets, and on the south side of the second rock was the third dam, the largest, probably about 250 yards long. I named these Middle Dam and South Dam, respectively.

When I finished marking their positions on the map I scanned the area around them carefully and quickly found what I had been looking for. Sneaking past the southernmost tip of the second islet, below the dam, was the creek that old Alec had marked on his map. I had not found it on my way in because I came through on the spring flood; now its course was clearly visible and it offered me an easy pathway once I had explored its route. Since the incoming water entered the lake from East Creek, the outlet became West Creek on my map.

When I had finished marking its location, I trained the glasses on the marshland north of West Creek and saw a fourth lodge, built just west of North Dam. Again I made a map note and returned to my survey. The rocky ridge to the north stopped short of the lakeshore; behind it was more marsh and in front of its easternmost point I noted lodge number six, a low mound of untidy, peeled poles that seemed to have a wide base. This was an old lodge, perhaps no longer in use, or used only as an emergency shelter. It had been built in very shallow water, close to a low mound of rock that sprawled toward the tiny, shallow bay where the mother beaver had intended to feed when the wolf killed her. I watched this inlet for a time with the glasses, but apart from duckweed and arrowweed and a few lilies, it offered nothing of interest; neither did the rocky finger that the female beaver had been crossing when she was struck by the wolf. I sketched these on the map, drew the outline of the other shallow bay that had been formed by the emergence of Alec's Point, and concluded my scan of the lake.

Behind me, I knew, lay the rock rise that led to Blueberry Flats, but I would have to plot it and the surrounding country by walking over it or, if I found a tree tall enough, by skinning up into its crown and getting a high view. In any case, I had done enough survey work for one day and my stomach was urging me down from my rocky pinnacle and on to the preparation of my lunch, even though the sun had not yet reached its noon position.

I scrambled down and walked to the tent and I stopped and listened for Paddy's expected cries. There was silence; I had to be stern with myself in order to restrain an urge to go in and lift the top off his lodge just to see if he was all right; thereby waking him up and precipitating an early feed. Instead, I lit a small fire, lowered one of my food packs, and took from it my slab of bacon and a bag of instant mashed potatoes. I was relieved to see that the bacon, though slightly slimy, was still fresh enough to eat.

After lunch, which was soon over, I listened again for Paddy and, failing to hear him, I took my fishing rod and tackle box and launched the canoe. I was going to try for a perch or two for my supper. When I was paddling toward Perch Bay, I remembered I had not crossed over to Water Lily Bay to see if I could locate any sign of a large animal that I had heard come down to the water to drink the night before, so I turned the bows and paddled across, entering the bay between Paddy's Island and Bass Island and aiming for a low, flat section of rock near where I thought the animal must have stood when it came to drink while I sat across the lake waiting to feed Paddy.

The light canoe put its bows gently on top of the rocky slope and I got out and dragged the craft out of the water. The area here was cloaked with alders and a variety of low bushes among which a few clumps of blueberries struggled for their share of light. Bur reed nestled at the water's edge and the rock surface a few yards from the shore was covered with a mixture of moss and coarse wild grass; here and there groups of devil's paintbrush were starting to raise their heads and some wild iris, great blue flags, would in time exhibit their delicate blooms not far from where I had landed.

I began to check the area for tracks, looking for telltale broken twigs, bent grass stems, and, raising my eyes, inspecting the gentle slope for sign of a trail. At first I couldn't find any trace of trail or tracks, but when I moved around a large clump of alders, the first thing that met my ground-inspecting gaze was the clear, large imprint of a bear's back foot, an almost human track. Soon I found others, some fresh, obviously made last night, others older. Backtracking, I traced the animal's route from the lake up to South Flats, finding numerous places where bruin had turned over large rocks in order to eat the insects that sheltered under them, especially the piquant, acidy ants. Quite obviously the bear came this way regularly and, like all his clan, never failed to investigate anything that might offer food along his route. With luck, I thought, I might be able to get a good look at him if I waited some evening on Bass Island, which was only a hundred yards from his watering place.

Satisfied, I returned to the canoe, launched it, and paddled toward the western end of the lake, intending to take a close look at the newly emerged dams and perhaps to run the course of West Creek for a little way.

Old Alec's Lake is about two and one third miles long by one and a half miles wide at its longest and widest places and occupies a total area of approximately five square miles; from Alec's Point to West Creek is about one mile, or perhaps a little more, but it took me almost an hour to cover the distance because I first crossed to the bulge of land near the second beaver lodge and spent some time exploring this area of marsh, inspecting the three lodges, and concluding that only the southernmost of the three, where the water was fairly deep, was still in regular use. This suggested that two beaver families occupied the region, the one claiming for its own the immediate area of the lake, including the big lodge on Paddy's Island; the other, less privileged colony living in the marsh south and west of the lake, its boundaries probably extending up to West Creek.

Knowing the territorial habits of beaver by then, I was fairly sure that the male who had sired Paddy, together with his now dead mate, had ruled the lake area for years, defending it vigorously against intruding beaver and expelling from their clan any of their own offspring if, by the time these reached young adulthood, their additional numbers threatened the well-being of the colony, which must always be maintained at the level of population that the territory's food supply can sustain.

This is the law of the wilderness, obeyed in one way or

another by all species except *Homo sapiens* and especially obeyed by beaver, who, like wolves and some other social animals, have acquired built-in birth-control methods that are activated when population numbers threaten the food supply. On these occasions, beaver produce fewer offspring—or none at all—by the simple expedient, enforced by the females, of refusing to mate, or, if they do mate, by somehow regulating the number of eggs that are to be fertilized. I was standing on top of the beaver lodge and looking over the marsh country when these thoughts occurred to me. I dug out my notebook and wrote in it a reminder to explore more fully at a later date the peculiarities of natural population checks, particularly as they applied to beaver and wolves, and to try to correlate the known factors that may account for this kind of elementary and necessary birth control.

I put away the notebook and climbed down from the lodge and got into the canoe. Paddling through the reeds of the marsh, guided by the gurgle of the creek, I passed South Dam, stopped just beyond it for a look at it, and then emerged from behind the thin curtain of cattails to find myself being slowly sucked toward the flowing creek. I let the canoe drift, steering with the paddle, and soon I was being carried downstream.

The current was sluggish, moving the canoe at less than paddling speed, and I was content to let the boat meander at will, now and then using the paddle to avoid contact with the rushes that lined the sides of the waterway while devoting most of my attention to the surrounding country. I would have liked to run the stream to the end of its course, but I couldn't that day because I had to get back to camp to feed Paddy; so, glancing at the sun moments after I entered West Creek, I determined the time was about one o'clock and I decided to allow myself an hour's run downstream.

I could not then be sure, but I estimated I was traveling some three hundred yards south of the channel I had used on

the first day to enter the lake and that the course of West
Creek would probably take me south of the knoll where I had
camped before I poled my way through the marsh. Digging
out Old Alec's map, it seemed to me that his memory had
failed him when he marked the creek, because he had placed
its entrance into the lake at a point midway between Alec's
Point and the first dam; in other words, about a mile north
and east of where it really was. This did not surprise me unduly. In all other respects the old man had been extraordinar-
ily accurate in drawing his map from memory. Only one error,
even if it was fairly important, was really better than I had
expected.

West Creek, running full with surplus spring water, cleaved
a route between the cattails which was as a superhighway
compared to the course that I had followed. On either side of
it the rushes ran north and south in serried ranks, but in the
fifteen-yard swath claimed by the creek for itself, there was
hardly a rush tip to be seen; I was confident that this stream
would provide good traveling for most of its course, once I got
to know the route.

The afternoon was warm, the marsh a place filled with
many attractions; all of them tempted me to stop and to look
and I resolved to halt my run and anchor the canoe among the
rushes and just lounge for a while. There would be time
enough later to do some serious exploring of the creek. Presently I felt drowsy and I lay down in the canoe, face to the
blue sky, intending to rest for a few minutes. Instead I fell into
a sound sleep.

When I woke up, the sun had traveled a good distance
across the sky and I was cramped and parboiled by the heat. I
had to get back to camp right away, for it was past the time for
Paddy's feed, a fact I was most conscious of as I portaged the
canoe over South Dam and pushed hard across the mile of
open water that separated me from Alec's Point.

I landed and approached the tent, and Paddy's wails assailed me, making me feel ashamed of my indulgence. I called to him; his cries immediately increased in volume and when I entered the tent I could hear him scratching wildly at the walls of his lodge. When I lifted the top off his house, Paddy shot out like a fat bullet and ran over to the sleeping bag, changed his mind, ran toward the north wall of the tent, wheeled about, calling excitedly and sniffing, and came waddling toward me. Evidently he had been so anxious to find me that he had quite lost his bearings when he emerged from the lodge. I stooped and held both hands out to him, the backs flat to the tent floor. Paddy hopped aboard and tried to crawl up my right arm as I straightened. As a result, he fell off and I had to make a quick grab for him before he hit the floor. I managed to get hold of his tail and quickly secured him in my hands again. I expected him to register fear, or at least to express vocal disapproval at the indignity. Not a bit. Paddy proceeded to repeat the experiment and I had to hold him with one hand while I lifted him with the other and pressed him to my neck, seeking to pacify him. He bit me. I had been aware of his young teeth, little more than hard ridges under his gums, but I had not thought that he could employ them to nip with. He didn't mean to bite in the accepted sense of the act, but he was so hungry that he just clamped on to the first warm, soft substance that he found, which happened to be my neck just below my right ear. It hurt. I snatched Paddy down to a level where he could not make his demands so immediately and effectively known and he at once tried to consume one of my fingers, taking half of it into his mouth and sucking it with vigor, occasionally chomping down on it with his teeth. That much I could stand; and I felt I *owed* him, anyway.

I thought belatedly about another problem. It would be almost impossible to leave Paddy in the tent while I prepared his feed, and it would be as difficult to turn him loose outside, for he would certainly wander away in his frenzy of hunger. I solved the problem by emptying my "possible bag" of its contents, slinging the strap around my neck and one shoulder, and stuffing Paddy inside and fastening the flap. He didn't like it; he kicked up a fuss, but he couldn't do much about it as I lit the fire and poured his milk into the pan. Three or four minutes later he was feeding, an undisciplined wild urchin who at first drooled out more milk than he ingested simply because he could not seem to settle down to purposeful feeding.

The contents of the first two droppers spilled mostly on my hands and clothing, but by the time I crammed the third one into his mouth, he had swallowed enough milk to take the edge off his giant hunger and he calmed down. About forty minutes later the milk pan was empty and Paddy had sucked his way through thirty-four droppers—a little more than four ounces—during an operation that was as tedious for me as it was delectable for him. I mopped him up, prodded his stomach gently, and felt relief when it responded to pressure. It must be understood that I had never before raised a beaver child and I had but the vaguest idea of the amount of formula that I should allow Paddy to have in one sitting.

My experiments were empirical of necessity and he appeared to be responding well, but it would be easy to do the wrong thing and kill Paddy with kindness, a concept abhorrent under any terms, but especially so now that he had wormed his way firmly into my affections. Like an overfussy but indulgent grandmother, I fretted over Paddy. Had I fed him too much, or not enough? Was the formula too strong, or too weak? Only time, I thought just then, could answer these questions, but in the meantime an exploratory poke at his belly indicated that it was not yet full to drum tightness—a bad thing—and not too flabby, either.

In the end, it was Paddy himself who answered the questions, not me. He searched for a moment or two after I had taken away the last dropper, a halfhearted performance, then he did what he had done earlier: turned on his back on my lap and promptly fell asleep, his mouth open, a little milk dribbling out of each nostril, and feeble snores emerging from his mouth.

I slid my hands under him and lifted him up. He wriggled experimentally, sleepily seeking to settle himself more comfortably, but he did not wake up. In the tent, he allowed me to put him back in his lodge and to cover him with some of the grass and ferns that had escaped intact during his scrambling around inside the chamber while I was away. Paddy continued to snore.

Seven About two weeks after I had rescued Paddy I walked to Blueberry Flats. It was intended to be a fairly aimless ramble undertaken as recreation but motivated by a measure of irritation because I had devoted so much time to nursing the kit that I had neglected my exploration of Old Alec's Lake and the surrounding country.

When I reached the clearing I stopped, not quite in the middle of it, and for no particular reason I stretched out on the ground and watched the sky. It was one of those soft spring mornings when the sun is clear and the blue heaven is just slightly hazed by thin clouds.

As I watched, I picked out the shape of a red-shouldered hawk that was circling slowly with stiff, unmoving wings and my attention became centered on the bird. It planed along, using the updrafts, making its display of aerobatics look simple; then it rose in tight spirals, became a dark dot, a tiny speck, and finally faded from sight. The sky was again empty. I lay as I had been, unmoving and entirely relaxed and feeling the warmth of the earth transferring itself to my body.

Slowly, with delicious care, I began to allow the living world in which I was wrapped to register on my consciousness, still keeping my eyes fixed on the endless blue above. From my position on the ground I began to notice sounds that were different from any that I had experienced before; the droning of a bee was louder and more purposeful when listened to in this way; the rustle of a dragonfly's wings became more personal now that I heard it from the ground; a small breeze swept through the grasses with the authority of a gale.

I lay completely relaxed, watching the sky and the cottontail clouds that scudded across it while I tried to absorb the scents and sounds that surrounded me. The experience was so pleasant that instead of lying there for the few minutes that I had intended, I allowed more than an hour to pass.

Quite by accident I had discovered a new part of the wilderness, and when I rose from the ground and turned back for home, I realized that in my own clumsy way I had experienced a little of what it is like to be an animal that, small on the ground, must live continuously in this low-level world and must encounter conditions that are far removed from those by which man is confronted. This sharpened my resolve to try as best I could to become a part of this beaver country in which I now lived; and to attempt whenever possible to expose myself to the same forces that influence the behavior of a wilderness animal. I knew, of course, that I could never put it all together, but I hoped I might be able to gain a little more under-standing.

It was only natural that I should recall Paddy, who was no doubt still asleep in his lodge, replete after a liberal meal of milk and water mixed with cooked oatmeal which he had eaten out of a tin plate, a simplification of his earlier feeding method that I found greatly relieving if a little messy. He always managed to smear the thick mixture all over his face and paws and on my sleeping bag, where he insisted on par-taking his meals. Despite my best efforts to change his dining locale to the tent floor, where the sticky mess would be easier to clean, Paddy had to date refused to budge, no doubt as-sociating his personal security with the now familiar odors that clung to the stained bag; and since he had responded so well to plate training, I was reluctant to become too arbitrary about the issue, electing instead to coax him into adopting a new eating place.

The change from droppers to plate had not come without a struggle. Paddy was a nursing baby and his mother's soft breast had offered him more than food; it was also a thing of security, and it was a sort of miniature punching bag that accented the pleasures of eating with the pleasures of nuzzling and paw pushing. The droppers were poor replacement for a mother's marvelous glands, but they did offer a certain amount of solace, and though my hand was not nearly as yielding as the breast, it was able to give some measure of comfort when the little beaver's spread paws pushed and flexed against it.

This arrangement worked well enough for a few days, but soon Paddy's appetite and body growth made dropper feeding an affair of tedium and frustration for both of us and I was forced to switch him to a plate. A time of trial ensued for Paddy. I mustered every bit of patience that I own in the face of my ward's vigorous protests, reminding myself during the two days of training that the kit was hungry and confused and entitled to make a fuss, but I was unable to become seriously worried about his condition, because of the strength and frequency of his wails and the power of his assaults on the logs of his lodge, which he gnawed with his baby teeth, making a distracting sound when I was trying to sleep. It was like living in a tiny wooden hut that was being assaulted by a giant termite.

The training was simple. After putting the food mixture in the plate, I dipped two fingers of one hand into the stuff and pushed gently on his head with my free hand, bringing his questing mouth into forceful contact with the food that adhered to my fingers. Though he sucked and licked at my digits almost every time he encountered them, he could not at first understand that the mixture was coming from the plate. His hunger was aggravated by the aroma of the food and the unaccustomed manhandling made him nervous. It speaks well of a beaver's intelligence that he managed to get the idea so quickly.

By the evening of the second day of trial, to my immense relief, he suddenly dipped his face into the plate and began to suck and lap, making some extraordinary noises and aiding himself by planting both front paws in the thick formula. Shortly after he had mastered the technique of plate feeding, I discovered his reluctance to be evicted from the sleeping bag. Each time I put the plate on the tent floor he ran up and down the sleeping bag searching frantically, wailing and looking at me in reproach, unable to understand my reasons for tapping his plate where it rested in the unaccustomed place.

Because I was so engrossed with Paddy during the first two weeks of our life together, I stayed close to the campsite most of the time and affairs in and around the lake progressed somewhat uneventfully. When I was not playing with my ward, or grooming him, or feeding him, I busied myself by improving my campsite, recording plant and tree species, and watching the beaver as they swam in the pond.

Halfway through the second week, I was pleased to notice that the lake beaver had become accustomed to my presence in their domain and were beginning to show a good deal of interest in me. On three occasions when I was late in feeding Paddy, a large beaver that I took to be the clan patriarch approached within a hundred feet of my shoreline when the kit's impatient wails were uttered. The buck was plainly interested. He swam up and down swiftly, raising himself high in the water and peering at the campsite. Was this Paddy's father? I believe he was, but of course I shall never be sure. His very obvious concern over the kit's cries strengthened my opinion, for beaver families are closely knit, small social groups whose members show individual distress if one of their number is injured or killed.

I was now able to confirm that the family I had been observing at my end of the lake shared the big lodge on Paddy's Island and was composed of a large buck, a smaller adult that I took to be a young female because of her special relationship with the patriarch, and three half-grown kits, probably born last spring to the old mother that had been killed by the wolf. It appeared as though the buck might in time take the female as his new partner, an event that would no doubt produce larger litters next spring.

I could not be certain of these things, but I felt there was merit in my suppositions, especially since the buck tended to wander alone for much of the time that I watched him, while the smaller beaver and the three young ones often went about more or less together, swimming in spread-out, ragged formation and usually feeding in the same places. This suggested that the male still grieved for his mate, perhaps not in the full sense of human grief, but in his own untamed fashion.

By the end of the second week, all the members of the family had become quite accustomed to me and showed no fear, even in broad daylight, provided I did not go too close to them. Indeed, they showed remarkable curiosity in me and in the campsite, though I was unable to decide whether this was elicited by Paddy's scent and sounds, or by my presence, or by all three. However it was, I took to spending half an hour beside the lake first thing each morning, sitting on a boulder by the water's edge, smoking my pipe. Nearly always the buck would soon appear on the surface and swim toward me, keeping about fifty feet from shore and circling in my vicinity as we scrutinized each other. Each time he did this I spoke to him softly.

One night, some three days after I had sprawled full length on Blueberry Flats, and while I was sitting by the lake watching the effects of full moonlight on the water, it occurred to me that it would be interesting to return to the flats and repeat the experience by night. After spending many nights in wild places, I well knew the change that occurs with sunset; the moods of the forest night are altogether different from the moods of sunlight and there are sounds and quirks of character during the hours between the two lights that totally transform the world of the sylva. No one who pretends to know the wildwoods can do so without tasting in solitude their dark hours.

The wilderness closes in at night. A commonplace daytime scene becomes an unrecognizable mystery after dark. Immensity shrinks, vision is lost, and sound is magnified. The eyes have little value and a lone man strains to hear in the bush dark and his nose, atrophied by misuse, begins to work again, to probe the odors around him with suddenly feral interest. All this I knew, but I had never before experienced the night from low level.

When I went to get a jacket from the tent I checked to

make sure that Paddy was asleep; then I left, following one of the well-defined game trails; the one I chose sloped down into a narrow valley and then ascended the rocky rise that eventually leveled off where the flats began.

When I reached the place where I had stretched out during daylight, I lay down, face to the grasses, and I gazed upon the forest of plant stems. From this position I encountered a jungle-like scene that limited vision to within a few inches of the eyes. This was the world of the small animals, dense and labyrinthine and restricting, even allowing for the special senses that these creatures possess and man lacks.

As I lay there trying hard to get the feel of things from the sensory level of a beaver or a hare or a raccoon or a mouse, I realized that smell and hearing at night are probably the greatest survival senses that an animal possesses and that vision is practically useless in such areas of interwoven stems and fronds. Here, for either hunter or hunted, caution must be always uppermost; what lies ahead, behind, above, and to the sides must be listened for and smelled out. This world of forest night must require perpetual alert for those small creatures that use it. Here even hunters are hunted. A raccoon is tracked by a wolf; a hare is stalked by a fox; a mouse is savaged by a weasel; a cricket is eaten by a snake; a weasel is pierced by the talons of an owl. . . .

Walls of waving, rustling green reach taller than the head and create sounds different from those audible from above the tops of the grasses. I was reminded, down there, of my passage through the beaver canal, when the cattails closed in over my head. I felt confined and confused at the time, but I knew I would eventually emerge from the maze. A small on-the-ground creature spends practically all of its time in this kind of habitat, day or night. I would not want to be small in such a place; I would not want to walk the wild earth forever surrounded by such obstacles.

I stood up, brushed off my clothes, and tried to ignore the itchy places left by half a dozen mosquito bites; these were small price to pay for the experience that had just been mine. As I walked home, I felt a greater sense of relationship with the wilderness and an extra measure of understanding of its animals, especially the beaver, which, clumsy land creature that it has become, must be particularly vulnerable to its enemies when it goes ashore to feed or to find a new home for itself.

Because of my own experience under the moon, I was most conscious of the perils that beaver face during their land travels and, reviewing the animals that I had watched on shore, I realized that most of them had been careful to stay close to the water's edge unless they were forced by scarcity of food trees in the autumn and early spring to travel inland. This was logical. At best, a beaver on land can run at about the same pace as a fat human being; they are absolutely no match for the larger predators on terra firma and so they distrust the forest floor, very much aware of the dangers. Tonight I could be truly sympathetic, for I had experienced at least something of what it was like to be small on the ground. Now I turned to go back to Paddy.

Eight I was almost out of food, including Paddy's milk and oatmeal; I had not yet cut a good pathway for myself through West Creek and the orphan beaver presented a problem in logistics.

There was no question but that I had to go outside and buy fresh supplies; there was equally no question but that I could not risk trying the West Creek route for fear of encountering delays that would leave both of us without food; and to clinch my problems, Paddy could not be left alone. I had to take him with me.

I sat in front of my campfire pondering these things and

listening to Paddy as he worked to demolish his lodge, a habit he had picked up during the last week and at which he now excelled; give him two more days, I thought, and the lodge I had so carefully made would be reduced to matchwood. The orphan had now been in my care for twenty-four days and he had grown lusty and his teeth were effective tools.

The transport of a young beaver from A to B may seem simple to those who live in proper houses in cities and towns where there are hardware stores that sell things like chicken wire and even fancy cages, but for such as me, encamped in the wilderness and faced by a canoe journey through thick marshland while transporting said beaver, the trip from A to B was far from simple. Though Paddy was too young to be left to his own devices while I was away, he was also too active to carry loose in the canoe, from where I was sure he would quickly dive into the water, a great fondness for which he had already acquired.

In the last ten days or so I had allowed him to play in the little channel eroded by the stream, and he loved it, provided I stayed near so that he could see me and smell me and hear me when he came up from under the surface. If I moved away, he immediately cried his plaintive little wail and came out of the water and ran—or perhaps I should say stumbled—after me, so that it was an easy matter to get him out of his long and narrow swimming pool when it was time to shut him up in the lodge. All I had to do was walk away, calling his name, and Paddy would bounce along like a well-trained puppy. Nevertheless, to make sure that he did not wander into the lake by accident and risk getting lost, I carried a quantity of dead sticks and made a sort of barrier at the wide part of the spring runway, just before it emptied into the lake. The water could run out, but Paddy could not get into the lake without either coming on shore, where I could see him and prevent his dangerous wandering, or climbing up and through my barrier, again giving me an opportunity to thwart his youthful explorations. So I knew he could swim. Self-taught, he was, from the very first moment that I allowed him to lower an inquisitive nose to the spring. He had sniffed at it, wetted the very tip of his nose, backed away in momentary panic, and then, licking the drop that spilled down his stubby chin, made a rush and belly-flopped into the water. Down he went, ungainly, a furred bundle made of arms and legs and tail that thrashed and churned wildly until it rose again.

He was certainly surprised. It was obvious, watching his expression, that he didn't know whether to cry in fear or to mumble in satisfaction and pleasure. In the end he did neither. He kicked with his little webbed back feet and swam upchannel until he got to where the spring fell in miniature cataract. There he played under the falling water, rolling, opening his mouth and drinking as though from a tap, and actually turning somersaults. A few minutes later he dived and I watched him kick his way downchannel and I became worried, thinking that he was heading into the lake. I had just about made up my mind to go in after him when he came up. I called him and he came to me, dripping and happy.

As was usual when I called him to me, he wanted to be picked up and fondled and played with, trying in the meantime to bite my fingers, but I would no longer allow him to do so, because his teeth had grown and he hurt when he chomped! Now, sitting up soaking wet and looking into my face, he demanded to be picked up. I stooped and took him into my arms and held him close and he nuzzled his round head under my chin and I scratched his wet belly and he mumbled.

Then he struggled to get down and he dived again into the water, came up, slapped his tail, and then paddled up and down the channel for a time, now and then diving and staying under for perhaps a minute. It was then that I discovered that he needed to feel the security of my presence. To see whether he would notice my absence while he was so enjoying himself, I stepped back a few paces and stood behind a young spruce. Almost at once Paddy left the water and crawled up the bank, crying his fear and sniffing frantically, searching for me with his nose. I came out of hiding, feeling foolish and sorry, and I called his name and he came as fast as he could and he asked to be picked up and he remained in my arms until he fell asleep.

I was naturally intrigued by his tail slapping; it told me that the habit is instinctive in beaver, for Paddy had not been able to learn it from any of the adults in the pond. But it suggested more than that. Paddy slapped his tail out of pure *joie de vivre*; not out of fear, but out of excitement. Is that how the habit became established? Was it that some ancestral beaver tried slapping the water for fun, found it pleasing, and made a practice out of it that later proved useful in startling lurking predators? Those questions, alas, remain unanswered.

At any rate, on the night of the twenty-fourth day "post-Paddy," I sat by the fire and slapped at mosquitoes and pondered the problem of transporting the beaver child by canoe to where my station wagon was parked. Imprisonment of my ward appeared to be the only alternative, but the choice of container was limited to my "possible bag," a canvas pouch that would not endure for long under the onslaught of beaver teeth. But if I slung it around my neck so that the imprisoned Paddy rested against my chest, I would probably be able to thwart his attacks on the canvas and keep him captive long enough to reach my destination if I paddled nonstop. I didn't like that idea too much. It would entail a long, tiring journey broken by few rests while eating cold rations and drinking water. It didn't make me feel better to consider that I did not know how long it was going to take me to retrace my route to the outside, despite the fact that the return journey would be made easier by my knowledge of the marsh. After about an hour of this solo debate, I decided to leave at first light in the morning, carrying Paddy kangaroo style and trusting in the bush gods to see me through. I went to bed, but not before I had liberated Paddy from his tattered prison and suffered him to crawl in with me. In a short time both of us were asleep, my ward secure in my company, I being confident that, as usual, Paddy would rouse me before dawn.

He did, by wetting me. It was pitch dark and chilly in the tent except for the spreading warmth of his wetness on my stomach. I groped for the flashlight and looked at the time. It was five o'clock and raining. It was one of those steady, soaking rains that is so good for the wilderness and makes things grow and lessens the risk of forest fires. But it was not what I wanted that day of all days. Lying inside the sleeping bag and fondling Paddy, who after doing the deed had slipped off my belly and now snuggled tightly against my side, I considered for some moments postponement of the journey out. I didn't even want to get up, preferring the warm wet to the cold wet that I would encounter once I got out of the sleeping bag. I dozed for a short time and was awakened again when Paddy crawled between arm and body and stuck his face into my armpit so as to suck at my shirt.

I got up. Paddy remained in bed. I took off my wet things and shivered as I found a warm shirt and a change of shorts and some heavy drill pants. Dressed, I lit the tiny alcohol stove that I have for rainy times and I boiled water; it was to be coffee for me, my last, and boiled oatmeal and powdered milk for Paddy. As the water heated I munched some raw oatmeal and a handful of dried fruit, then I made coffee, put oatmeal into the water to cook, and mixed Paddy's milk with warm water. When he, too, had breakfasted with his normal gusto and splatter and I had finished my first cup of coffee, I left him in the tent while I went outside to get the canoe ready. The rain was fine, but just as wet as a heavy fall.

Back in the tent, I dug my rainsuit out of my duffel bag and found my broad-brimmed canvas hat. Afterward I packed my remaining food supplies, wrapped them in a small square of canvas, filled a two-gallon plastic jug with fresh water, and stored the lot in the bows of the canoe. I returned for Paddy and my "possible bag."

At first he thought it was a game and he kept sticking his head out of the bag while I was trying to fasten it, but when I at last incarcerated him inside, he got rough. He called and wailed and gnashed his teeth and scratched and jumped about and just generally made himself a pest while I was collecting two paddles (one should always have a spare for safety's sake) and my push pole, the poplar I had cut the morning that I found Old Alec's Lake.

By the time that I pushed away from shore Paddy was fit to be tied. And I mean that literally—I gave the matter serious consideration. You who read this have probably not attempted to paddle a canoe while a frantic small beaver bounced inside a canvas bag and swung himself back and forth, somehow managing to deliver several well-directed kicks at your solar plexus; at least, I hope you haven't, for your own sake.

Paddy made me angry. I wanted to stop paddling, whisk him out of the "possible bag," and give him a couple of good swats on his sleek, fat rump. But I didn't, of course, for he would not have understood and I don't believe in physical punishment anyway. Nevertheless, my ward's antics had to be stopped or I would have to abandon the journey. And then I got my inspiration.

I had noticed that Paddy quaked in fear every time the red-shouldered hawk flew over us emitting its piercing, two-syllable whistle. Why not imitate the hawk? I did, managing it well enough to intimidate Paddy, who became quiet at once. So began a journey that is as unforgettable as it was brutal, a seventeen-hour marathon that went on endlessly throughout all of that gray, wet day. Initially, the biting flies and Paddy's periodic fits of rebellion kept me occupied, if not diverted, but as the hours passed, my muscles began to protest, mildly at first, then with an intense refinement I would not have credited. Toothache all over the body! Paddle for fifty minutes, rest ten minutes . . . monotonously, forever, with my kit wailing and fearing and finally becoming numb with fatigue and anxiety. My brain became foggy, my will hung to purpose by a thread. And then it was over.

It was midnight when I got into my station wagon. I was too tired for more action; so was Paddy. I can't remember going to sleep, only waking up at eight o'clock next morning, when I fed Paddy, skipped my own meal, and drove away. One hour later I was in a store buying provisions while Paddy explored the inside of the car. The rural emporium, one of those good old country stores, was warm and smelled of good things like coffee and tea and bananas, which I craved, and kerosene and fresh bread and chocolate and new denim and piquant baling twine and cheap scented soap and even hanging flypaper—you know the kind, those sticky spiraling affairs that entice flies and then keep them stuck to the stuff with which the hanging strips are coated. The ones in that emporium had attracted many flies, very many flies; and some buzzed and fought valiantly to free themselves and others buzzed and fought not at all and some had given up all things days earlier. I loved just standing in the center of that store, eyeing the shelves and smelling the delicious odors while I said pointless and even banal things to the magnificent old crone who ran the place, an ancient body with the face of one of the witches of *Macbeth*, wrinkles and warts and all, but a lovely woman who generated a personal warmth far exceeding the cube of her sere little body.

I was bone weary and my right shoulder and wrist ached from continuously giving directional twist to the paddle, for I am a right-handed canoeist and would rather suffer than alter style for anything but fleeting changes of pace; I wanted sleep more than anything else, except, perhaps, six bananas, eaten one after the other; ripe bananas, the almost black kind that when peeled reveal a delicate, gooey, enticing yellowness that tickles the taste buds and demands salivation. I also wanted to talk. I had not conversed with another human for almost one month and the luxury of receiving a reply in my own language was a deeply sensual experience. The words didn't matter, or the theme; just to talk one to one with another human soul was more than pleasure. It is always thus with me. I never seem to forget how to talk during my wilderness trips, and it doesn't matter whether I am gone a week, a month, or six months, my desire to gab seems to be as strong every time. But then, I confess that I am somewhat garrulous.

By the time another hour had gone by I had a stack of cartons and paper bags of food which included six boxes of mixed-cereal Pablum and one box of rice Pablum for Paddy—the rice was for loose-bowel times, if any—and a twenty-five-pound bag of powdered skim milk. In all, I must have bought over a hundred pounds of food, which would last us at least twice as long as my first load and would present few problems now that I was going to return in an otherwise empty canoe.

After I paid for the supplies and spent a few more nice minutes chatting with Mother, as she invited me to address her, I transferred the goods to my wagon, pushed Paddy down between the front and back seats, and drove away.

One more hour passed. Paddy had eaten a banana, skin and all, and I worried about it. I parked the car on the county road, curled up on the front seat after giving Paddy another banana, and went to sleep worrying about him all over again. It was midmorning and time was wasting, but I had to sleep.

I woke up and found it dark. Paddy had also awakened and was demanding food; it was his calling that had nudged me out of a deep, beautiful sleep that I was loath to give up, even though my legs were stiff in all joints because they had been kept for so long in the knee-bend position on the front seat of the wagon. I switched on the interior light as I sat up and looked for Paddy, who, when last seen, had been eating a banana on the floor; now he stood upright on the back seat, eyeing me in a fashion that was as close to a glare as a beaver is capable of giving.

He was hungry. So was I. Pablum and milk and water for the beaver imp; coffee and bananas for me, three of them; they are my favorite fruit and my one dietary extravagance, so I don't feel guilty when I indulge, which isn't all that often.

Tonight—for I discovered it was two o'clock—Paddy would have to eat his supper cold. I mixed the milk in the water and added the Pablum and put the tin plate on the seat in front of the little glutton. Would he like Pablum? Of course, it was a stupid question and I was almost certain of the answer before I asked it. The makers of the baby food may not be at all aware of it, but they have discovered an elixir that pleases the gourmet that lies just under the surface of wild animals. I had fed squirrels, raccoons, otters, bears, deer, moose, chipmunks, nestling birds, skunks, white-footed mice, two wolf pups, and one baby porcupine on Pablum; they all loved it with gluttonous abandon. Now Paddy joined the group. He stuffed his face into the dish and sucked and he didn't stop until he was nearly choking for lack of air. I left him mumbling and wheezing and sneezing out some of the mixture that got up his nose and I went outside to light a small campfire for my coffee water. While I was gathering sticks I ate a banana with almost as much gusto as Paddy was sucking up his supper-breakfast.

The night was clear and full of stars, but no moon. The night was also full of mosquitoes! Hordes of them, big and little, and all as hungry as Paddy, but it was my blood they were after. I dived back into the car and sprayed myself with OFF!, forgetting in my anxiety for protection that the pressurized contents are highly irritating to wild noses. Paddy sneezed a good slug of his mixture over one of the car windows; he continued to sneeze and blow, still trying to eat his meal, which put the stuff on the back seat of the car and not a little of it all over my head and face.

I took the OFF! container outside and finished applying it to myself, using it liberally. Now the blood suckers didn't bite, but they continued to buzz around me, ever on the alert for an opening. I put a match to the fire, filled my mess tin with water, and put it on to heat, balancing it on a flat rock. I ate another banana.

By the time I had worked through my second cup of coffee and ingested my third banana, it was getting on for three o'clock. Paddy had forgiven me for making him sneeze and lay placidly snoozing on his seat. I left the shelter of the car and picked up the canoe from where I had left it among some alders and carried it to the small landing place, where I set it down upright. I returned to the car. Paddy snored.

I looked at the sky through the windshield. Polaris twinkled as ever, clear and bright; my guide. I would leave just as soon as I had packed the canoe and stuffed Paddy into his prison bag, for I wanted to get home as quickly as possible, return to my observations, and give Paddy his freedom and the run of his beloved spring. I was also anxious to build my ward another lodge, a bigger one; and I planned sneaky things with a roll of chicken wire I had bought from Mother, so I could leave him for longer periods and expect to find him in the same place when I returned home.

During the many trips between car and canoe, Paddy gave no signs of caring. He was fast asleep, oblivious; but he returned to struggling wakefulness when I started putting him in the "possible bag." We had another tussle and I did my hawk thing and he shut up, not knowing that hawks do not fly at night. I would have done an owl, too, but I can't hoot worth a darn. I got under way.

I traveled cautiously through the darkness, keeping Polaris just slightly off my port bow and watching for deadheads and other obstacles as I followed the big, fairly open marsh that would bring me to the beaver canals by about first light, if I didn't take a wrong turn. To my relief, Paddy gave up struggling and fell asleep, no doubt as tired as I was by the first trip.

The night sky was magnificent, a fitting crown for this beaver country through which I was quietly passing. For a time, I amused myself by picking out stars and constellations, using Ursa Major as my guide. The Big Dipper's pointers, of course, led me straight to Polaris, although I had no need of them to find the brilliant star of the north. Polaris, in turn, led me to Ursa Minor; there was Draco and Cepheus and Cassiopeia and over to the west glowed the constellation Perseus accompanied as usual by the stars Mirfak and Algol. And thousands upon thousands more shining orbs gazed upon me while the Milky Way sent down its glow to give a measure of sight to my eyes.

After an hour I let the canoe drift and I rested for ten minutes. There was a hint of light in the east and I could detect the outlines of trees and cattails. An owl hooted, frogs filled the night with their chorus, the mosquitoes, ubiquitous little brutes, sang their monotony in my ears. A beaver surfaced near me; I kept still and it swam to within four or five feet of the canoe and gave it not a glance. It paddled slowly toward an area of nodding cattails that were vaguely visible on my right. I took up the paddle and set off anew.

Nine The canoe slid onto my rocky beach on Alec's Point at six o'clock the next evening, fifteen hours after I pushed away from the county road. I had made better time returning because I was now much more familiar with the route, but I was exhausted when I staggered out of the boat and hauled it further up the shore. And I was hungry, and so was Paddy. The poor mite had only ingested one banana and a skimpy dish of Pablum since his large feed the night before and he had spent most of the fifteen hours cooped up in the bag—with periodic airings in the confined space of the canoe.

It was surely nice to be home! Paddy thought so, too. I

liberated him by the spring before I did anything else and he
scampered into the water as quickly as he could run and he
dived and rolled and slapped his tail for all the world like a
human youngster emerging from school on the last day of
term. I watched him at first, but because he seemed oblivious
of my presence, I thought it would be all right to go to the
canoe and begin my unpacking and tidying up.

Every now and then I looked toward the spring to make
sure that Paddy was still there and each time I saw that he was
fully occupied in his water play. When I had taken about half
of my load up to the tent, I quite forgot Paddy in my pre-
occupation with the task in hand. Naturally, I was anxious to
be done and to make supper for both of us and then go to bed
and I didn't think again about the kit until the canoe was
empty.

Suddenly I remembered Paddy and I looked for him. I
couldn't see him. I ran to the rivulet and scanned the clear
water. No Paddy. I looked around, in vain. I ran to the lake
edge and searched for him on the surface. He was gone. Lost.
I called his name loudly, repeatedly, realizing at that moment
how much I had come to care for the friendly, funny little
animal. The thought of Paddy lost somewhere in the darken-
ing marsh and getting picked off by a predator was too hor-
rifying to contemplate. I called and called, standing by the
lakeshore for several minutes; then I turned abruptly, meaning
to go to the canoe, to launch it; as I did so I stumbled over
something that was immediately underfoot. I flailed my arms
to recover my balance and I heard a wail. I had stumbled over
Paddy. There he was, soaking wet and injured more in his
feelings than anywhere else, just scrambling back up to a sitting position, his nearly flat tail spread out behind him like a
scaly black shoe sole.

I scooped him up from the ground and cuddled him against
my neck, and he mumbled and nibbled gently at my Adam's

apple. I rubbed him all over while I looked down at the rocky shoreline to see a wet trail of small, duck-like footprints leading out of the lake water and ending where I had stumbled over my ward, who had escaped the confinement of the spring, entered the lake, and had responded obediently to my calls. This made me angry with myself. I should have kept my cool; I should have retained the objectivity of the field naturalist and observed calmly as I called for the kit; then I would have found out some things that now were lost to me. How far away had he been? Had he just surfaced and come directly to me on hearing my voice? Or had he resisted my call, tempted by the full freedom of the lake?

Paddy mumbled. Darn it all, anyway! I could not find it in me to be objective and calm if I thought my beaver child was in danger. Paddy now meant a lot more to me than a few observations that I would most probably make at some other time. I carried him to the tent, unzipped the doorway, and put him inside. He curled up on my sleeping bag, soaked as he was, and I didn't mind a bit that I would have a wet bed tonight. I went outside and made our suppers and within a half hour we were both asleep, Paddy, as always, snuggled beside me. I remember that I dropped off with one hand on the beaver's head; he was sucking my little finger.

Just before dawn the next morning Paddy began to mutter for his breakfast. I was still tired out, but I got up, made him a plateful of his food, and gave it to him; then I went to bed again. When he awakened me the next time the sun was high, the inside of the tent was hot, and I had a raging thirst and a big hunger. Also, I was stiff, especially in my right shoulder, arm, and wrist, and I had a blister on the inside curve of my thumb; but none of this was too surprising after having paddled for almost thirty-six hours with not enough rest. Yet I felt good.

It was nine o'clock and the day was beautiful. I would stay

home, lounge, play with Paddy, listen to the birds and the frogs, and watch the dragonflies consume their own weight in mosquitoes, cheering their efforts each time I saw one of the iridescent insect hunters make a basket out of its legs and scoop up a blood sucker. The pesky blackflies had thinned down to a spotty rear guard, for which I was truly grateful, because these tiny humpbacked insects are probably the worst pest to be encountered in the northern wilderness.

When Paddy finished his Pablum and milk, I let him wander at will around the campsite, keeping an eye on him, of course, but making no effort to restrict his explorations. I estimated he now weighed about four pounds and he was getting more coordinated every day and was also losing some of his baby nervousness. During the morning he went into the lake three times while I, feeling nervous, watched. The first time I let him swim out for about twenty yards before I called. He turned and came back to me at once. The second time he dived and I almost went in after him, but he rose quickly and swam parallel to the shoreline for about fifty yards as I walked along the water's edge. When I thought he had gone far enough, I began to retreat, calling his name. He looked my way, saw me moving back, and at once left the water and hurried toward me.

I took him for a walk inland then. We walked behind Spring Rock and down into Deer Valley for a little way, and Paddy nibbled at tender grasses and explored many things. I was glad to see him eat grass; it was the first time he had shown interest in anything but his formula. On impulse, I unsheathed my bush knife and cut down a tender willow sproutling. After making a couple of slices in its young bark, to make the sap flow, I called Paddy, and when he came to me I bent down and showed him the willow. He sniffed it, stuck his tongue out and licked it, and took it from me with his mouth. He held it for a moment, put it down, picked it up again, and placed one front paw beneath the stick and one above it; he began nibbling it, making small incisions in the bark, and he twisted the stick with his paws, rather like someone eating a cob of corn. I watched intently and realized what he was doing. Instinctively, dipping into some hidden, mysterious reservoir of knowledge, Paddy knew just how to eat a stick.

I had thought he was eating as he twirled, but I was wrong. What he did was to cut a little notch in the bark while he held the stick steady with his paws; then, grasping one edge of the split bark with his teeth, he twirled the stick, the bottom hand pulling toward his body while the top hand pushed away, neatly rotating the willow; as the stick turned, the bark imprisoned by Paddy's teeth stripped away from the wood and when he had pulled an inch or so free, he ate it, retaining his hold on the sproutling. In this manner he nibbled off about eight inches of the bark before something else attracted his attention. He dropped the stick, waddled away a few feet, and stuck his nose into a small cluster of wild strawberries.

The fruits were not quite ripe, but he ate three of them and consumed two of the tooth-edged leaves. Now he started to groom himself. He had done this before, but it was the first time I had seen him do it in the open and he was much more thorough than during those other occasions in the tent, going over most of his body with care, scratching and combing with his split claws, and enjoying every minute of it.

I called him to me when he had finished and I picked him up and carried him back to camp. When I put him down he walked to the lake and entered the water and swam a good way out; he floated on the surface for a few minutes, then turned and swam back and scrambled ashore. To my surprise, he walked to the tent, sat down beside it, and began to groom himself all over again.

When he was finished I picked him up and carried him

inside the tent, for I knew his habits by now; he would sleep for the next couple of hours, perhaps longer than that because of the long, difficult experiences of his trip outside. I planned, while he was napping, to start building him a bigger and more substantial lodge at the edge of the spring, near its source where the water had eroded a pool that was about three feet deep and some six feet in diameter. This place was ideally suited for my plans and would provide a good, safe home for Paddy when I was away from the camp.

With the roll of chicken wire I had bought at the store, I intended to fence off an area some ten feet square, placing the wire *inside* the fence posts to stop Paddy from chewing them down and fastening the mesh with stovepipe wire instead of staples—which I had forgotten to buy. I felt this would be a good arrangement once I had built a lodge that was large enough and heavy enough to shelter Paddy and to protect him from any possible predators, especially bear.

Paddy was more than willing to curl up and prepare himself for sleep. This entailed several turns of his fat little body as he sought the most comfortable spot; having found it, he flopped inertly and totally relaxed. For some moments he kept watching me, as though to make sure I stayed until he dropped off; then he yawned twice, his eyes lidded, and he slept. I left the tent, closed the doorway, and got out my tools.

The first task was to dig a hole on the bank deep enough to allow the water to enter and wide enough to accommodate the base of Paddy's new home. With my small war-surplus entrenching tool—one of those folding shovel-picks that infantrymen carry—the job took almost an hour, even though the ground was comparatively soft. Now I was ready to cut the logs I would need, and as I collected ax and saw and walked to Deer Valley, where there was a good number of poplar trees the right size for my needs—between four and six inches thick at the butt—I itemized all that I knew about the construction of a beaver lodge.

Years earlier, I had asked Old Alec if he knew how beaver built their lodges, but he couldn't tell me. I asked several other people, with equally negative results, before I gave up questioning and resorted to observation. It took almost three years before I was rewarded with the correct answer. As is so often the case in field studies, I came by my information unexpectedly when I stopped beside a beaver pond in the early autumn of 1958. It was a lovely September morning and I had walked some five miles on a day's trip to a small lake where I knew I would catch a supply of perch. The pond was about a mile away from my destination and when I reached it I sat down and sipped coffee from a thermos. It was while I was doing this that a beaver rose to the surface twenty yards away and swam quietly to a long, low hummock that jutted out of the pond. Cattails, water plants, and scrubby land growth interrupted my view of the animal when it climbed ashore and waddled among the plants, but in a few moments it returned and began to inspect a place opposite from where I sat, an area of water that appeared to be about two feet deep and in which the beaver swam intently before it stood upright, its shoulders, front legs, and head protruding out of the water. It stood thus for a time; then it ducked under the surface.

My curiosity was idle; I wondered what it had been up to, but I was not greatly intrigued, my mind more intent on fishing than on the casual antics of one beaver that had come and gone so quickly. But five minutes later the water roiled at the same place and I was able to detect the shape of the beaver. It was doing something under the surface. Now my curiosity was roused. I got the field glasses and looked. Sure enough, the beaver was evidently intent on some important purpose. Now and then part of its body momentarily rose out of the water, but the animal's forequarters and head remained submerged. In a few minutes it left again and the water in its wake was considerably stirred up and clouded with mud.

That beaver made me give up my fishing trip and sent me home late that evening, ravenously hungry, fascinated by what I had seen and determined to be back at the pond at first light the next morning. I had been fortunate to be present at just the right moment to watch a beaver begin construction of its lodge: I had seen the animal inspect the proposed site, find it acceptable, and then go to the pond bottom to begin the tedious task of carrying mud with which to build the base of its lodge.

Trip after trip the beaver undertook to the pond depths, each time returning with an armload of mud or stones. Slowly, it built up the bottom in the shallow place, a patient, tireless workman who in just over three hours made forty-one trips, each averaging slightly more than four minutes; the longest trip took nine minutes and the shortest a minute and a half. In this time, the beaver packed mud and small sticks and stones to a height where its base protruded nearly a foot above the surface of the water over an area that I judged to be roughly six feet in circumference.

Now it began to work on top of this more or less oval mound, making numerous trips for larger sticks and branches, almost all of them old, peeled food poles, which it dumped on top of the mud base. By evening the untidy mound rose about three feet out of the water and spread over an area some seven feet wide at the bottom; it was slightly narrower at the top.

When I returned the next morning the beaver had advanced still further with its lodge, and now it had a companion, another animal about the same size, though I could not tell the original worker from its mate. I judged this to be a young adult pair either constructing a new home for the first time together or building a fresh lodge because the old one was untenable. Overnight, one or both animals had heaped more sticks on the pile, which now reached a height of about six feet.

That day I continued my observations while the two animals worked and I learned how simple their techniques were: First, build a mud base so that it protrudes the proper height from the water, this height being governed, I believe, by the animal's knowledge of the water table in its domain, *or* by the beaver's confidence in its ability to control the water level in the pond. Either way, the mud platform must form the floor of the lodge. When the floor is brought to the proper height, the sticks are piled on top of it, in a seemingly careless and haphazard fashion. Watching, I could not at first understand why the animals were building a *solid* lodge, but that was undoubtedly what they were doing. Stick was piled on top of stick, any way at all; there were no hollow spaces left to furnish a chamber, just an interlocked pile of poles and branches now and then weighted down with stones and tied in here and there with pond weeds and other bottom debris.

By the end of the second day, however, I understood the technique. After the animals had erected their now conical superstructure to the desired height—and I do not know what determines this height—they ceased working out of the water and dived under the surface. From this time on I saw them only when they came up for air, but by then I was fairly certain that they were digging and gnawing their way into the massive cone they had built.

Later I was to confirm that this is exactly how beaver build their lodges. After the mound is built they start chewing and digging underwater, making at least one tunnel, sometimes two or three, at the ends of which the main chamber is hollowed out. In this way, the "bedroom" is above water level, it is well protected by the interlaced mass of sticks and debris that rest on it, and it is usually equipped with more than one escape hatch should some animal attempt to dig into the lodge from above, a thankless task for any predator, even the strongest.

When the tunnel or tunnels are finished and the chamber shaped to the right dimensions, usually between two and three feet in diameter and about two feet high, the beaver's home is ready for occupancy, but the animals continue over the years to strengthen their lodge, first plastering the outside with mud and small sticks, then as time passes adding to its outside bulk, so that eventually a lodge may reach twelve or more feet in height, be about twenty feet wide at the base, and have a bedroom four or five feet wide.

A beaver begins its plastering by sweeping together a quantity of mud from the bottom or from the edges of the pond and clutching this load between its arms, pressing it against its chest. Now it swims to the lodge, climbs out of the water on its hind legs, and, steadied by its wide tail, easily steps up the side of its structure to the work site and tamps in the load with its hands and sometimes the top of its nose.

The air vent on top of the lodge is not actually a hole, as might at first be supposed, but consists of a spot that has not been covered with mud so that the interlaced sticks within the mass allow air to enter the chamber and exhaled gases to emerge. In some lodges the interior sticks are more loosely spaced than in others, but in none of them is it possible to look down into the chamber, no matter how intently one stares. I have tried it many times, as I did when I was searching for Paddy after I had found the remains of his mother, but always my eyes have encountered the same maze of sticks obstructing vision beyond the first few inches. But it *is* possible to hear the beaver in their lodge, especially after the young are born, when their little cries and occasional mumbles are quite audible if one puts one's ear near the vent.

In winter, the snow on top of the lodge is often yellowed

from exhaled breath, and although it may appear as though the white blanket has entirely covered the mound and thus excludes air, closer examination reveals at least one small hole in the snow, melted by the warm air rising upward from the lodge chamber; or, in extremely heavy falls of snow, one finds a hollowed space under the white that contains enough air for the colony.

Exactly why beaver shape their lodges in the form of a cone is not known, unless it is that the design is naturally suited to the purpose, offering strength, stability, and ease of construction. It seems fairly evident that the knowledge required to build lodges and dams is inherited or, as some would say, instinctive.

I am never quite sure what is meant by the word "instinct." It is really a non-word, which functions to dismiss the unexplainable by use of a convenient, if somewhat unsatisfying term. I feel that use of the word leads to oversimplification. If an animal is seen to behave repeatedly in a certain fashion, sometimes performing a complex task for which there is no quickly evident explanation, one is at once tempted to say that the animal is governed by instinct, a word derived from the Latin that simply means that the creature is *impelled* to act in a particular fashion. This does not (for me) explain either the forces or the mechanics of such action, so the mystery remains to tantalize. How is an animal programmed to perform a special task for the first time? How much of this *instinct* is built in and how much results from the effect of outside influences?

Deer Valley is a pleasant place. It is a long, narrow ravine carpeted by grasses and wildflowers and made cool by plentiful aspens, oaks, and maples that cast welcome shadows, but open enough to allow good visibility and easy walking. It begins north-northeast from the water's edge at the small point of land where the wolf killed the mother beaver and ends against the flanks of a steep granite scarp some three miles distant from the lake. I christened it Deer Valley because of the many deer tracks I found imprinted on it, though the game trails that crisscross its surface show the prints of many other animals, including wolf and bear. The lower end of the valley, just behind the place where Old Alec built his cabin, is but five minutes from the place where I set up camp, and there I stopped to cut my logs for Paddy's lodge.

Of course, I could not build a home for the kit with the same skill or in the same proportions as his parents had done, but I was confident that I could produce a reasonable facsimile that would offer almost as much protection as the real thing. This second lodge could not be built with a removable roof, if it was to be attack-proof, and would thus not allow me to reach Paddy when he was "at home." This no longer mattered; he was large enough and active enough to come out when he was hungry and vocal enough to attract my attention when he wanted me. Also, I felt fairly sure that he would respond to my voice if ever I wanted him quickly, which turned out to be the case.

It took me less than an hour to cut down and trim enough trees for my needs and almost another hour to carry them to the building site by the spring, but by lunchtime I was ready to start the building and by the end of that day Paddy's new home was finished. The next morning I sharpened the fence posts, drove them into the ground with the ax, and fastened the chicken wire to them. I had built an enclosure that would keep Paddy from straying and a refuge that would ensure his safety, even if a bear decided to smash through the flimsy chicken wire. If danger threatened, I could rely on my ward's nimble wit to cause him to dive into the water and swim into his lodge, the walls and roof of which, I was positive, would resist the efforts of even the largest bear.

When I first contemplated the task of building the lodge, I had viewed it with some misgivings, thinking that it would entail a great amount of work and that the end result would be a flimsy structure; however, at the end of the third day, when I put Paddy into his nursery and watched him examine the boundaries of his new home, I felt greatly pleased and rewarded.

I had started its construction after I drove four cedar stakes deep into the ground, one at each corner of the hole that I had dug at the edge of the spring and which had quickly filled with water. On top of the stakes I built the floor of the lodge, using poplar poles instead of mud, but covering the platform with a good, thick layer of gumbo and troweling it smooth with my entrenching tool. Built into this floor were two holes, each about a foot square, one in front, facing the stream, and one behind, some eighteen inches away from the bank into which I had dug. The floor was three feet by three feet, not oval like a true lodge would be, but satisfactory and much easier to build that way. Now I had a platform furnished with two exit holes that led underwater to the stream.

On top of the platform I made a tepee of logs about four feet high, fastening them together securely with wire, and then I began to pile logs and branches and dirt and rocks against and on top of this. When I had done, the lodge stood almost six feet high, had a base of over six feet, and was so laden with sticks and stones and other debris that it was virtually impregnable. I climbed on it and jumped up and down, I kicked at it, I rammed a pole against it. It stood firm. Now I started to plaster, filling in chinks, and at last I ended up with a strange, *almost* conical mound that resembled a beaver lodge to some degree, complete with top vent. I was proud of my lodge.

I went to get Paddy, arousing him from one of his many naps, and I put him inside his enclosure. Of course he investigated immediately. At first he climbed up one side of the

lodge, as though inspecting its construction. Evidently it met
with his approval. He descended, walking on his back legs and
holding his hands pressed against his chest, a soft but continuous mumble emerging from his almost-closed lips. At the
water's edge he dived and I saw the outline of his body as he
swam toward the underwater entrances to his home. Soon I
could hear him moving inside, especially when he nibbled
appreciatively at the poplar bark that I had deliberately left on
the logs to encourage him to feed on his own.

I watched for an hour. In that time Paddy amused himself
by exploring once more the area of the spring, by inspecting
the wire fence and nibbling at it tentatively, and by going in
and out of his lodge chamber. Now I could relax. The kit had
shelter, security, lots of good clean water, and about a hundred square feet of land in which to grow up undisturbed. To
celebrate, I decided to take a trip in the canoe.

I glanced occasionally over my shoulder as I walked to the
rocky beach, but Paddy showed no interest in my departure.
He was much too busy having fun, every now and then climbing ashore to nibble halfheartedly at some green tidbit or
other. Maybe now he wouldn't need so much Pablum and
milk.

I set out for West Creek, intending to explore its course and
clear from its path any obstructions that might hinder the passage of the canoe, for I was most anxious to trace the route of
this waterway. If possible I wanted to avoid another brutal
journey through the canals and marsh, although I would not
again need to take Paddy outside with me when I went for
supplies because I was sure he would be fine in his new enclosure. Nevertheless, I could not be away from him for too
long and so it was important to find the shortest and easiest
route out, for both our sakes.

Two hours after I entered the creek I was amazed to exit

from it into the main body of the marsh at a place that I recognized and which was no more than two hours away from the county road where my car was parked. From camp to car in only four hours, and easy going at that! Now I could do the trip in one day and, if I left at first light, be back for supper. Satisfied and feeling very pleased, I turned for home. But my euphoria quickly passed, for it was characteristic of me that as soon as I had solved one problem I began worrying about another one. I had left Paddy alone and outside for a long time. Would he be all right by the time I got back to camp? Would he still be inside his pen, or would he have dug his way out and gone into the lake? I paddled harder, unable to stop from worrying and taking little notice of the wildlife of the marsh and creek.

It was late afternoon when I got back. Paddy was nowhere to be seen. I called and I waited for Paddy to come out of his lodge. He did, almost at once; and as soon as he saw me he began to complain, demanding his supper and running up and down inside the wire. I reached over the three-foot-high fence and picked him up. He struggled and cried and made his hunger and reproach clearly felt. I chuckled as I took him to the tent and put him down while I started his supper, and for the first time Paddy dogged my heels, getting underfoot and making a nuisance of himself in his anxiety to get his Pablum and milk. Experimentally, I mixed perhaps a third less of the formula than usual, thinking he might have already helped himself to some green food. I was right; but this did not prevent him from gorging until his stomach was distended and the tin plate was licked clean. He didn't demand more, and I would not have given it to him had he asked for it, for fear of upsetting him. After the meal he became torpid, so I let him sleep in the tent, but I picked up my bedraggled sleeping bag and put it out of his reach. It was time that he learned to sleep elsewhere and more than time for me to have a dry bed. Tonight I was going to put him back into his playpen to see if he would be content to remain there until breakfast time.

I sat in the darkness without a fire, smoking my pipe and listening to Paddy's splashes as he played in his nursery, where he had spent the last three hours. It looked as if he was prepared to stay there for the rest of the night. Earlier he had slept on the tent floor for two hours before waking up and calling to me, mumbling until I went in and picked him up and carried him outside into the near dusk. When he had had enough of rubbing against my face and neck while I caressed his belly, he signaled that he wanted down. This meant that I was to put him inside his pen, which I did, much to his satisfaction. There were some green poplar tops left over from my lodge building that I had stacked near the fence and I picked up one of them and put it inside the fence. At once Paddy came to explore. He sniffed at the tree, nibbled at some leaves, climbed through the branches, and then settled down to munch on one of them, quickly cutting it in two. The piece he had severed was about eighteen inches long and not much thicker than a pencil and a few leaves grew from its end. Paddy tugged it to the water, swam out with it a few feet, and dived, carrying it inside his lodge. Presently I heard him working on the branch. I left him and sat in my usual place, watching the darkness arrive and listening to the changing sounds of the wilderness. One by one the day birds roosted and quieted their voices; one by one the nighthawks flew and dived and called and competed with the first hesitant whippoorwills.

Tonight there was a quarter-moon. It hung like a slice of silver melon, "catching rain," illuminating the lake with a soft light that made for fair visibility. I was protected in some measure by OFF!, and the mosquitoes were not too troublesome, especially since the ones that were not discouraged by the repellent were nicely kept away by the tobacco smoke. I sat quietly for an hour, noting the arrival of a beaver that came close to shore and then swam slowly toward Perch Bay. Was it Paddy's father come to check? I wasn't sure.

The wolf howled. He called forlornly from the direction of Blueberry Flats, his voice so loud that I felt sure he must be sitting on the edge of the open space nearest to the campsite. From the distance came an answering howl. His mate? Perhaps not. Maybe it was another wolf somewhere. The wolf's voice continued to haunt the night for three or four minutes, his singing alternating between long, deep *wooo-ooo*s and shorter, sharper calls. Afterward, silence.

Ten I don't know when bannocks were invented or whether the Scots or the Anglo-Saxons made them first, and it doesn't really matter, but if there is one thing that caught on faster than any other when the first white settlers came to North America it must be this staple, simple-to-make bread. It was one of the mainstays of the pioneers; to people like myself it still is. The name derives from the Anglo-Saxon *bannuc* and the Gaelic *bannach*, but whichever way you say it or spell it, the end result is usually good to eat.

One morning during the third week of June, while Paddy was disporting himself in his nursery, I decided to treat myself to a stick bannock for breakfast, though, as usual, the coffee was first. When it was ready I squatted by the fire, sipping, and prepared my bannock mix.

This is my recipe for stick bannock: one cup of water, two teaspoonfuls of baking powder, a pinch of salt, and enough flour to form a stiff ball while stirring. When the dough is stiff enough, make a snake out of it, or a rope if you prefer. At any rate, stretch it until it is about twelve inches long; at this point, if you have used enough flour, it will be about two inches thick. Now cut a stick two feet long, heavy enough to support the bannock; it is best to find a stick that has a convenient thin branch emerging from the main stem. Trim this branchlet down to about two inches in length and make it pointed. Put a point also on the end of the stick. Take the snake of bannock and wind it around the stick, spiking one end of it on the trimmed branchlet and the other end on the sharpened point. Now, over a hot bed of coals twirl your stick bannock; when the dough is nicely golden brown all around, it is ready to eat, preferably hot, but I also eat it cold, for I usually make enough to last me all day, enjoying the hot bannock in the morning and making do in the evening with the leftovers.

Another recipe that I like produces pancake-like bannocks. Mix a half to one teaspoon of salt, according to your taste, and two tablespoons of baking powder in two heaping cups of flour and stir in enough water to form the bannock dough, which should be fairly stiff, so you can lift it with the fingers. Put the bannock in a greased pan, if you have grease, and set it over a bed of hot coals until golden brown; turn it and do the other side and you have a large, tasty bannock good for three meals for the likes of me or enough for breakfast for two others. For variety, put in less salt, add sugar to taste, and pop in some freshly picked berries, such as wild strawberries, blueberries, saskatoons, huckleberries, or what have you. And another recipe makes dumplings: mix as before and drop dollops of bannock dough into a stew—marvelous, rib-coating stuff.

I made my stick bannock and baked it over the hot coals, broke it into three pieces, and spread some tangy marmalade on one and began my breakfast. That's how my day started. Bannocks and lots of sunshine and Paddy enjoying himself in the spring water; I thought that life ought to be able to go on exactly like that, forever. I sat over coffee and watched an oriole fly past carrying a fat bug to his lady; a catbird mewed at me from a nearby shrub, and a big bullfrog who sat on the edge of the water directly under one arrowweed stem, like a castaway on an island where only one palm tree grew, was singing his moo-song with glee, but pausing now and then to flick out his sticky tongue and capture a passing insect.

Somebody once said: "Some people sits and thinks and some people just sits." I wanted to "just sit" that morning, but stray thoughts intruded persistently and played musical chairs inside my head, so that when the male beaver showed up as had become his habit at this time of the day, I gave in to my mind and allowed it to become fixed on one thought. The buck suggested the theme when he landed about one hundred yards from me and ambled to a place where a small, untidy mound of debris had been raked up. The beaver climbed on the mound and sat on it, tail folded under his seat as though he didn't want his backside to come into contact with the materials of the little hill.

These haphazardly built mounds found around beaver country are usually located close to the edge of the water, and many people who have studied beaver believe that they serve as territorial markers on which the animals belonging to a particular family deposit some of their musk as a warning for other beaver to keep out of their area. This explanation is too facile for my liking. It is, I feel, as unsatisfactory as the reason given for the tail-slapping habit, which, because it contains an element of truth, becomes acceptable to the degree that most observers do not seem to trouble themselves further over it, saying, in effect: "The slapping is done as a warning; ergo, let us now dismiss it, for it is no longer of interest."

Indeed, for a busy biologist this may well be an excusable attitude. After all, to some people, solving the riddle of the tail-slapping habit may appear to be of minor import when there are so many other seeming imponderables to consider. But not to me. I want to find out all that I can about the tail-slapping behavior of the beaver and I want to find out all I can about the little mounds that this animal builds on the borders of its ponds and, if at all possible, I want to acquire this knowledge without resorting to explanations suggested and clouded by my own, near-cybernetic civilization, which all too frequently causes me (and others) to make judgments that result exclusively from the influences of my man-made, *un*natural habitat.

Here are a couple of "fer instances": In my world of ambulances, police cars, and, quite often, wars, the wail of a siren instantly causes alarm: *that is the only intent of a siren*, it is man's special toxin that probably began with the blowing of a conch shell or the beating of a stick on a hollow log. Similarly, in this contrived human environment, frontier markers serve as warnings to other nationals; implicit in these border cairns is the very real threat of war should others insist on invading our sovereignty.

Sirens and border cairns are easy to understand because we make them for very specific purposes and they each have one use only, and a grim one! But things are not nearly so simple in the world of nature, no matter how much we would like them to be. True, animals resort to warning devices and to "keep out" signs, but these do not usually result from deliberate, planned reasoning and are more likely to occur as a side effect of an anterior, naturally sensible action.

The beaver slaps water to attempt to clarify a doubtful situation, as I have explained. For the same reason the buck deer snorts sharply and suddenly when unsure, and the hare pounds the ground with stiffened front legs, and the wolf woofs softly but suddenly, and the bear does the same, and the hunting owl screams harshly in the silence of the night. And what hunter has not been made to jump out of his skin by the sudden, deliberately explosive escape of a ruffed grouse? This bird can move over the ground as silently as a ghost and can fly "normally" with little sound; if possible, it resorts to stealth to avoid an attack, crouching quietly, well camouflaged by its woodsy-brown feathers; but if a predator approaches too closely, the bird explodes into sudden and noisy action. As often as not, this puts a hunter off his mark.

All such actions have been designed by nature as primary aids for the survival of *individual* animals. If, as a side effect, other animals of the same species (or of other species, come to that) take warning from the tail slap, or the deer snort (or what have you), all well and good, but this is not necessarily the intent of the reflex actions. The warning element is just a felicitous benefit to the others if they are experienced enough and sufficiently intelligent to *interpret* the alarm. Similarly, some animals are intelligent enough to know that the sound is too distant to affect them or that they are themselves so placed that they have no need to be fearful, such as a beaver swimming in an open pond, able to dive instantly and escape in this way.

In like manner, the so-called scent mounds of the beaver may well provide only coincidental boundary markings—and not very important ones at that! I once put this suggestion to a biologist friend, who became positively angry at my temerity in questioning "an accepted fact." An argument followed. In the end he exclaimed: "O.K., smart aleck, give me one good reason to account otherwise for the scent mounds." I did, and there is now at least one biologist in North America who agrees with me.

To even begin to understand the scent-mound theory, one must first examine the beaver's glands, two pairs of which are located under the skin between the back legs. The first, the oil glands, appear to serve a definite, single purpose: to furnish oil with which the animal waterproofs its coat; these glands may do other things as well, but if they do, I cannot imagine what they are and I am willing, for now, to let the matter rest there.

Next to the oil glands are found the castor, or musk, glands, said to exist for marking territorial boundaries with their pungent musk and to signal sexual readiness at mating time. In large animals, the musk glands may grow to the size of an orange and together may weigh as much as four or five ounces. Inside the glands is the thick, orange musk fluid, pungent-smelling stuff, but not offensive to my nose.

At one time the castor glands were prized because it was believed that their extract, or the dried, ground-up gland, could be used to cure a variety of illnesses, but today their main use is in the manufacture of perfume and they have fetched as much as twenty-eight dollars a pound for this purpose; they are also used by trappers, with more or less success, to lure beaver to the set.

Castor musk, by the way, should not be confused with *castor oil*, that heavy medicine inflicted on patients as a purgative, which is obtained from the castor bean, otherwise known as *Ricinus communis*.

I can readily accept that beaver musk does serve in some measure to define the boundaries of a family's range and I can also agree with the sexual-attraction theory—during the breeding season the glands contain more musk and drip this out in larger amounts—but I find it hard to accept the mound theory. This is because beaver of both sexes continuously discharge musk and oil in more or less measure during all seasons; both pairs of glands empty into the rectum and their contents adhere to the tail and parts of the animal's fur, especially around the groin and back legs, from where, when a beaver oils its coat, quantities of musk are also transferred to all other parts of its body.

In this way a beaver leaves a constant trail of musk wherever it walks or sits on land, and though this scent is faint to the human nose, it is quickly detected by the keen nose of another beaver. In other words, the animals ring their territories with a constantly renewed trail of musk, the odor of which, presumably, is individually distinct and instantly recognized as "family" by all clan members or labeled "alien" when deposited, or encountered, by strangers.

Under such circumstances, why should a beaver go to all the trouble of scraping together a mound on which to deposit its musk? I do not believe that it does. Rather, I lean to the theory that it makes its mounds for another purpose altogether and that because it then sits on them, often for comparatively long periods of time, the little hills become heavily impregnated with the musk and the oil that leaks from the beaver's glands and thus may *additionally* serve as boundary markers.

What is the other purpose? The beaver is clumsy on land—all observers readily agree to this fact—and it is built *low to the ground*, from which position, as I experienced during my experiment on Blueberry Flats, vision and hearing are somewhat impaired. It would make sense if a beaver scratched up a mound on which to sit during the day or night when grooming, resting, or feeding on some special tidbit, such as a succulent water-lily root. With the addition of six or more inches of height to its own stature, a beaver would be the better able to see, hear, and scent; it would feel more secure, sitting there on its raised platform so close to the water's edge. But what of the mounds themselves? What are they composed of? On examination, they are found to be made from a mixture of mud and sticks *and* decayed vegetation; if they are opened, one often encounters heat within the pile, the warmth of decaying organic matter. In addition, it is usual to note on the very top of the mounds pieces of sere vegetation, such as leaves or parts of lily roots and shredded grasses.

In daytime I have seen beaver sitting on these mounds, sometimes quietly enjoying the sunshine (seemingly, anyway), at other times grooming themselves, yet on other occasions feeding, and though I do not wish to offend those who adhere strictly to the territorial-marker theory, I must continue to believe that the mounds are feeding-grooming stations where a beaver can relax more fully because it is better able to rely on its guardian senses.

Paddy's mumbling took my attention away from musk glands and boundary mounds. I turned to look toward his compound and it was just as well that I did so quietly, for not five feet from the south end of the fence was the buck beaver, stretching his nose toward the wire and sniffing at Paddy, who stood on his hind legs close to the fence and sniffed back, mumbling the while. The buck was clearly hesitant, but obviously intrigued—as I was.

The buck knew full well that I was there; he had seen me and scented me often enough. But although he had of late showed very little nervousness when swimming near me in broad daylight, so that I was encouraged to think that I was slowly winning his confidence, I had certainly not expected him to land, walk past where I was sitting, and approach Paddy's nursery so openly.

For what was probably not more than a minute, the two beaver faced each other; then the buck moved forward a couple of short steps and by stretching put his nose against the wire. Paddy reached forward also; their noses met. The buck reared back at once and hissed loudly and gnashed his teeth. The effect on Paddy was instantaneous. He dropped to all fours, crying his alarm, and he backed from the wire. The buck did not hiss again and he didn't move from where he stood. I believe that the hiss and the champing of his teeth had been an unwitting reaction to the contact with the kit, which must have offered a variety of strange odors to the adult: Pablum, my own scent, perhaps some traces of the strong smell of the tent canvas. The buck would need more time to accustom himself to these things. I watched closely. Paddy stopped wailing and was mumbling again, more softly and insistently than I had ever heard him do it before, but he did not come closer to the wire. The buck moved a little nearer and stood on his hind legs. Now Paddy was the one to hiss and gnash his teeth. It was a pitifully weak imitation of the other's warning, but the little beaver was clearly telling the male, his father, that he was going to stand his ground, that this place was his territory.

The buck dropped back on all fours, turned toward the water, hesitated for a moment, looked my way deliberately, and ambled away to disappear under the surface of the lake. He rose some thirty yards out, swam a circle, and headed south, toward the dams and West Creek.

When he had gone, Paddy called me. He mumbled loudly and came to the wire as soon as he heard my voice. He became quiet; I picked him up and cuddled him and scratched him while he lay in my lap in his favorite upside-down position; he closed his eyes and went to sleep.

The short encounter between Paddy and the beaver that I was sure was his father gave me a great deal to think about and created a split in my emotions; that part of me that is the naturalist wanted to examine the meeting of the two beaver in the disciplined manner of science, but the other part of me, the romantic human, was much more preoccupied with anthropomorphism, hoping for a happy reunion between father and son.

This kind of thing happens often to me. I find it so easy to become involved personally, to relate with the animals that I deal with, and, in truth, I am glad that I do, but at times it can be something of a problem to separate the observer from the humanist. There is, however, a form of compromise to which I have often resorted that has so far furnished a solution to this kind of dilemma; I allow the naturalist first go at the problem, pushing the other self into the background, and when the matter has been coldly examined and milked for all it's worth, I allow the second me to take a hand. Surprisingly, often both viewpoints contribute to the whole—rather like a debate during which distinctly different opinions combine to establish a truth.

That morning I summarized what I had seen and I attempted to interpret the actions of Paddy and his father, deciding in the end that the buck's visit suggested that Paddy and the pond beaver would eventually come together, that the kit would find his proper place within his family and live in Old Alec's Lake until overcrowding demanded that he set out to find a pond or marsh for himself and to find, also, a mate. If all went well with him and the area did not become part of some trapper's line, Paddy could have a long life ahead of him. I wanted to believe that he would.

Once more I would have to face the sadness of having to part with one of the orphans that came into my care; I became attached to all of them, but Paddy had really squirmed his way into my affections. In any event, I was anxious about the kit's future. Would the buck kill him when I released him? Would Paddy know how to survive in the wild? Would he be strong enough? Could I teach him all the many things that wild mothers so naturally teach their growing young? Would he know how to cut down a tree? This ability of the beaver appears to be learned. The young watch their elders at work and begin to imitate their cutting actions, starting with small trees and working their way to larger ones. Of course, they have the right equipment and they are quite able to cut up small branches and sapling trees without any apparent "instruction," but to tackle a grown tree is another matter and requires a more complex technique, as I have described.

While these thoughts bothered me, Paddy dozed in my lap, supremely unaware of my problems and entirely satisfied just then to accept me as his parent. But one day, I knew, I would have to relinquish my hold on him and give him his freedom. I abhor the idea of pets and zoos, and I believe strongly that to be born free entitles an animal to die free, even if its life is short and its death painful. It is *not* better for an animal to live as the pampered darling of some human, ingesting the wrong foods, deprived of the pleasures of total freedom, robbed, in time, of the very will to be independent, and eventually, because of the frustrations of captivity, developing aberrant habits that perhaps culminate in the biting, literally, of the hand that feeds it, following which the darling becomes a menace and is either destroyed or shipped to a zoo, there to live dull and listless until death arrives tardily and ends the misery.

I have never imposed this kind of life on any of the animals and birds that I have helped in emergency. I never shall. Paddy would get his freedom just as soon as he was able to survive, and in the meantime, I would try to teach him as much as I could.

Eleven

Paddy and I were picking berries on the Flats under a broiling sun that was proving too much for both of us. We had spent an hour among the thick bushes that were now, at the beginning of the second week of July, bursting with sweet, purple fruit that I could strip off the branches a handful at a time into the small pail that I carried. Paddy, meanwhile, munched fruit, twigs, and leaves with indiscriminate appetite.

It was midmorning during a day of unclouded skies, heavy heat haze, flying vultures, and the continuous buzz of an army of cicadas; and flies (let me not forget the flies), the inch-long horseflies with their deep, painful bites that produce little gouts of blood, and the persistent deerflies, always trying to crawl into the hair and deliver their own powerful sting. Next to these two pests the remaining mosquitoes of the summer were as nothing, a nuisance rear guard that worried and sucked blood, but that was, thankfully, less active during the heat of this day.

I judged Paddy to be about six weeks old at that time, and as I watched him busybodying in and out of the berry bushes, more often than not wanting to eat the very fruit that I was picking, I felt amply rewarded for the trouble I had taken to raise this orphan. The wilderness has always been generous to me, giving me peace and comfort and understanding and the kind of pleasure that contributes to the growth of the mind. Looking at Paddy that morning, I had the feeling that the bush gods approved of my behavior, that I had paid back a little of what I owed. Call it an illusion, if you like; say that I am being fanciful. But if you ever find yourself sitting quietly and alone under the forest moon while staring into the coals of your fire, remember what I have just said and reflect upon the presence of the bush gods.

The little beaver had more than doubled his size and he now weighed, I thought, about seven or eight pounds. Recently he had become self-assured and confident, yet he continued to respond to me, exerting a measure of natural independence, but always glad to come when I called and enjoying as much as ever those moments when, cradled against my neck, I would scratch his head and belly while he nibbled at me in delight.

That morning, early, we had begun to swim together. It happened when Paddy entered the lake, remained on the surface, and set his course for Water Lily Bay. He became so engrossed with his journey that he did not heed my calls and I became worried. I went for the canoe, meaning to paddle after him and bring him back, but on an impulse I stripped off my clothes and dived into the water. By stroking hard, I caught up with him about five hundred yards from shore, in deep water, and when he realized that I, too, was in the lake, he gleefully began a game the rules for which he made up as we went along.

First he swam to me and scrambled on my bare back. His strong nails drew red tracks on my skin and his weight on the back of my neck made swimming difficult. To dislodge him I dived and swam beneath the surface, but I was no match for Paddy underwater. He dived more quickly, passed me on the way down, turned, and came streaking up again, his body a dark torpedo in the brownish water. I turned on my back, a position that allows me to watch the surface and which I always enjoy. Paddy avoided my kicking legs and rose above me, so that I had a marvelous view of him from beneath, a unique experience for me and one which has probably not been shared by many other people.

As I started up, Paddy aimed himself down and I feared he was about to collide with my head, but at the last moment he steered away from me and curved his tail downward. This sent him into a steep dive; I lost sight of him. But before I reached the surface, he was back up to my level, keeping right alongside me. We both reached air at the same time.

I took a deep breath, dodged Paddy's attempt to scramble on my back again, and dived once more, going deep, breaststroking as hard as I could. At some three feet from the cluttered bottom and with the pressure of the water making itself felt in my ears and nose, I leveled off; as I did so Paddy hove into sight, slightly in front and to one side of me. Now I swam in a direct line, keeping my depth. The young beaver paced me easily. It was a wonderful opportunity to study a swimming beaver underwater.

Paddy swam with both arms pressed to his chest, body outstretched, tail level but still, just trailing. His webbed back feet, so like those of a duck, were doing all the work, kicking alternately. To test his steering I moved to the right, making my turn slowly, watching him.

His right foot slowed perceptibly and he accelerated the tempo of his left foot, steering easily this way and keeping right alongside me, but still slightly in the lead. By this time I needed air, so I began my ascent, controlling my upward drift and inwardly "panting" my lungs, a trick I learned as a child skin diving in the Mediterranean Sea, when I discovered that if I forced my lungs to move by sucking my diaphragm in and out and expanding my chest repeatedly—with mouth tightly closed, naturally—I could get extra underwater time. I have never worked out the principle of this action, but I presume that the panting movement of the lungs allows unused oxygen to find its way into the alveoli. Anyway, it helps.

As I rose, I watched Paddy, who was no more than eighteen inches from my eyes. He curved his tail upward and rose quickly in this fashion. After churning a couple of playful circles on the surface, Paddy broke away, slapped his tail, and dived. I followed, but I could not see him at first. Then he brushed underneath me, close to my chest; I felt the fine touch of his fur.

We must have spent a little more than half an hour enjoying ourselves in this manner when the exertions of the swim warned me to go to shore. I called Paddy and allowed him to scramble on my back, where he clung, painfully for me, and hitched a ride all the way to the shallows. There he jumped off, dived, and came up thirty feet away, in deep water again. I walked up the rocky beach and squatted, calling him. But Paddy wouldn't come back. He stayed thirty or forty feet from shore, at one moment swimming in circles, at the next making short dives, and during all this performance he slapped his tail repeatedly. By now he could make quite a noise when he performed this action, for his tail had lost its roundness (the tails of baby beaver are not as flat as those of adults, being somewhat plano-convex in shape).

While Paddy was swimming, I got the glasses so I could watch his actions more closely; I wanted to learn as much as I could about a beaver's swimming habits. As I watched I made notes and I kept an especially sharp eye on his tail, because I had read in several books that beaver swim by moving their tails up and down, just as I had read that muskrats use *their* tails only for steering; but I had thus far failed to observe a beaver using its tail as a paddle while swimming on the surface.

Paddy used his tail to guide himself up or down and he also used it to help steer left or right when he wanted to make a fast turn, but I had not seen him use it in any other way, and I never did. Now, watching him on the surface, I noted that he swam like all the other beaver I had observed, kicking with his webbed back feet. Today I am still unable to confirm that beaver help to propel themselves through water by vertical undulations of their tails. Perhaps they do under some circumstances, but if so, it has completely escaped my observation.

I was about to put down the glasses and call my ward in, for I wanted to return him to his nursery before I set out to explore the country north of Blueberry Flats, when I noticed that Paddy suddenly became agitated. He turned for shore, slapped his tail twice in quick succession, and started toward me as fast as he could go. Something had obviously startled him, but I failed to detect anything out of the usual on the surface. At first I couldn't understand why he had not dived on becoming alarmed. Then it occurred to me that perhaps one of the other beaver from the pond had come near him *under* the water. When Paddy was less than halfway home this suspicion was confirmed.

Right alongside him the water roiled and the head and

shoulders of the buck came into view. I was on the point of yelling and dashing into the lake when I stopped, forcing myself to be calm and objective, for this was, finally, the moment of truth. Would the buck attack Paddy? The buck in the meantime had fully risen and was swimming alongside Paddy and not more than two feet from him. I watched.

Paddy cast one quick look at his father and redoubled his efforts, visibly increasing his speed but staying on the surface. The buck raised his head and shoulders higher. He moved closer to Paddy. Only about one foot separated the two animals.

I stood on shore clamping my jaws tightly shut, clenching my fists impotently, and fighting the urge to go to Paddy's assistance. The buck moved closer to my kit. Paddy called then, his baby wail of fear. I took the five steps that separated me from the water and I prepared to dive in.

The buck looked my way, edged nearer to Paddy. Now their bodies were touching and Paddy turned his head toward the buck and he hissed, but the male beaver seemed to ignore the threat and he kept his place. In this way the two traveled a further five or six yards; then the buck reached forward and nudged Paddy with his nose—a gentle push, really. He did it again, this time touching the kit on the neck, just behind the head. Now Paddy slowed slightly. He didn't wail.

Another few yards of distance closed. Still the buck showed no signs of aggression. It was more as though he was escorting the kit, touching him every so often with his nose, staying very close to him, but making no threatening gestures. Slow relief flooded through me and I stepped backward, watching intently.

When the two swimmers were some ten feet from shore, the buck moved away, toward the right, dropped back, keeping his head and shoulders out of the water, and let Paddy go the rest of the way alone. He watched as the kit scrambled ashore and ran to me, mumbling loudly as he raced for my legs.

I picked Paddy up. His heart was fluttering wildly. The buck stayed on the surface for a few more minutes, swimming very slowly eastward, then he dived, quietly; he just arched his brown back and submerged, leaving a rippling circle on the surface. I stroked Paddy and talked to him, telling him he had been foolish, that his father had meant him no harm. The kit responded to my voice even if he couldn't understand the words. He calmed, nuzzled into my neck, nibbled at me painfully, and then asked to be set down. I put him in his nursery, watching him for further signs of fear, but he seemed fully recovered. He swam in the spring for a few minutes; then he dived and disappeared into his lodge. It was almost three o'clock, his siesta time.

I set out ten minutes later, carrying the field glasses and my compass, en route for Blueberry Flats and, I hoped, wolf country, an area north and west of the Flats from where I had heard nightly howls during the last ten days, some of them high-pitched and uncoordinated. Unless I was much mistaken, the wolf cubs were up and about. It would be marvelous if I could find the den.

As I walked, I recalled the recent meeting of Paddy and the buck. Moment of truth indeed! For Paddy and for the buck and for me. Now I was convinced that the big beaver meant the kit no harm; if he had wanted to, he could have killed Paddy long before the kit even realized his danger. The buck could have come up underneath the kit and grabbed him by the belly and dragged him down, either drowning him or ripping out his intestines. Instead he had surfaced, swum alongside Paddy, and nuzzled him much as Paddy nuzzled me. Although I knew I would never be able to prove it, what I had just witnessed convinced me that the buck remembered Paddy and that he still felt the bonds of relationship.

The problem from now on would be to get Paddy to trust the other beaver as he trusted me, to transfer his love for me back to those to whom it rightfully belonged. In the process, I hoped, the kit might retain some affection for me. It would make it easier if he did; it would help me in the days ahead, when against my innermost feelings I would begin to push Paddy away, to slowly reject him so that he would turn toward his own kind. The time was not yet come, but it soon would.

I carried these thoughts for a time; then I made myself think about the wolf pack that I felt sure was rendezvousing not far away. Maybe I would be lucky enough to find the pack's summer range and catch sight of the family.

The big wolf had made several kills around Blueberry Flats in the last three weeks, including at least one deer. I had found also the remains of five grouse, a fox, and two raccoons. He evidently was a good provider, judging by the fact that the kills he had made near my campsite represented, in all probability, only about 25 percent of his total needs. By now, almost certainly, the bitch would be hunting with her mate, so they would probably range farther afield and perhaps manage to take more deer, an animal that, unless it is old or sick, is usually too fleet for one wolf to hunt down.

Sometimes it is possible for a patient, experienced tracker to track a wolf to its den by following spoor and other signs, particularly if the country over which the animal ranges is fairly open and dotted with marshland, at the edges of which the ground takes readily to footprints. But I was not too confident in this area; there were many tracks of all kinds leading in all directions, and although the wolf's big imprints were easy to identify when I found them, his course was erratic. He loped hither and yon as his nose, eyes, and ears instructed him, checking a chipmunk burrow here, a raccoon hole there, lifting his leg against a stump or a rock, going any which way and at times appearing to be traveling in two directions at once. It took time and much careful scrutiny to read the story of the wolf's travels. At one place, about thirty feet from a veritable giant of a white pine, I came across a curious scene that, for a change, was easy to interpret. The wolf had caught a porcupine in the open and had charged at it, but he had stopped short and, the tracks suggested, just in the nick of time, before he got a faceful of quills.

Porcupines are even slower on their feet than beaver, but whereas the beaver caught away from water has little chance of surviving a wolf attack, the quill pig becomes a dangerous foe when it stops at bay. Slow it is when walking, but stopped, with stiffened front legs and its club tail swishing back and forth, the porcupine develops unexpected agility. Its defense technique consists of a fast swivel on its front legs, between which it tucks almost all of its quill-less head so that only its top and the round, bulbous eyes are visible. In this position it pirouettes like a dancer and meets with its tail each charge that an attacker makes.

The army of quills that stud a porcupine's back and sides are effective weapons against a sudden body bite, but the docile animal's heavy, quill-studded tail is its real weapon. By meeting an attacker "tail on," the porcupine ensures that it is always ready to deal a heavy blow to the predator's head, face, or if the hunter is foolish and inexperienced, right into its open mouth. Should the porcupine manage to do this, the fight is over and the hunter flees the scene, leaving its intended victim free to seek sanctuary in a tree. The hunter dealt such a blow stands little chance of recovery, with a couple of dozen sharp, barbed quills buried in its tongue and gums. Death when it comes under those circumstances is usually a happy state.

Wolves often succeed in outfeinting a porcupine by simply circling it and making frequent charges that are checked just before contact with the powerful tail, until the porcupine gets tired and slows his fast swivel turns. Then, at exactly the right moment, the hunter darts in and grabs for the quill-free head; if it succeeds, the game is soon over. Biting hard and pulling backward at the same time, the wolf drags the victim until one or more fangs fracture the skull and enter the brain. Then a quick but powerful swing of neck and head throws the porcupine into the air and onto its back, exposing the unprotected belly. The wolf feeds, eating its quarry from the belly inward, leaving most of the skin and quills.

Dissections of the cadavers of trapped wolves have shown that this animal is able to stay healthy with a number of quills stuck in its stomach lining and esophagus, despite signs of irritation around each lesion. I have seen wolves on five occasions kill a porcupine in the manner described after duels that lasted from fifteen minutes to almost an hour.

On two occasions I have seen dog foxes attack porcupines, a vulpine trait that I have not seen mentioned in any book that I have read on the species. But on each of those two occasions the porcupines escaped when the foxes evidently decided that their prey was too dangerous. It may be that foxes do not normally hunt porcupines or, if they do, that they usually attack young and smaller animals, which are less dangerous than adults. Perhaps the two foxes I observed mistook for young ones the adults they tried to kill. But it seems unlikely that a fox, even a large one, could successfully subdue an adult porcupine. Some may try, as did the ones that I saw, but they are probably wise enough to give up before they get a faceful of quills.

Studying the marks of the battle between the wolf and his intended prey that were etched on a patch of bare, dusty ground, I was able to piece together much of the action, though I could not tell how long the confrontation had lasted. The wolf had charged repeatedly, his tracks said. And the porcupine had met every charge with his tail. The ground where the porcupine had stood at bay was swept in a full circle by the stubby tail, leaving marks rather like those that would be made by the bristles of a stiff broom and here and there losing a few quills, which I collected from the miniature arena. Where the porcupine had maneuvered on stiff front legs was another, much smaller circle of disturbed soil, while outside of the defensive ring the wolf's tracks always stopped just out of reach of the tail.

Eventually the hunter gave up. This suggested that he was not really hungry, for he had caught the porcupine fair and square out in the open, in a place where there was absolutely no cover and no convenient tree for the quill pig to climb. Undoubtedly, had he really wanted to, the wolf could have killed the animal. As it was, his tracks left the scene; about ten yards from the site of the duel, he had stopped just long enough to give a couple of contemptuous rakes at the ground with his back paws before loping away toward the northeast. Examining the ground more closely, I was able to follow the porcupine's small tracks to the foot of the white pine. Looking up, I saw the creature, sitting on a large branch some twenty feet from the ground, staring down myopically, but otherwise unruffled. I guessed the fight had been recent, maybe only an hour ago.

I left, following the wolf's trail, which was again becoming indistinct. For fifteen minutes I cast about in a zigzag manner through thick forest, over rocks, into small clearings, and eventually coming into sight of a beaver pond that I did not know existed. It was a large one but I could see only one lodge on it. The pond was about two miles from my camp, located almost due north and sitting in a cup that was made by rising granite that girdled the water for more than three quarters of its shoreline. The only place not closed in by rock was a narrow valley of marshland where a curved dam was located.

For a time I lost interest in the wolf while I climbed a tall pine and checked the surrounding country. From my perch I saw a second pond, about half as large, linked to the first by the thin strip of marshland. I was to find out later that these two ponds, which I named East Pond and West Pond, were fed by several streams and that the beaver in the larger, East Pond, pretty much controlled the water level of West Pond, at the eastern edge of which they had built a second, smaller dam. Scanning West Pond with the glasses, I saw two lodges, one located at the northeast corner and the other at the southeast, beside which was another dam, quite a small one, that led to another low and marshy area.

When I was on the ground again, I returned to my quest and looked for wolf sign, but now, on the rocky terrain, this was difficult to pick up. Here and there I found places where the wolf had left his mark; twice I spotted the track of his maimed foot, but I could not follow his progress any further. I was, however, in the general area where I thought the howls came from, so I decided to continue exploring for a while longer, working my way northeastward around the first pond, toward an area of thick spruces that grew on a ridge. I had seen this place during my tree survey and it looked to be the most likely wolf country; it offered good cover for the cubs and might well be the place where the dog and his bitch had decided to rendezvous for the summer. I thought the spruce forest to be a little more than half a mile from where I first saw the two ponds.

Now I walked as quietly as possible and I stopped often to scan the ground and to listen, not expecting to hear the adult wolves, but hoping that I might perhaps hear the play noises of the cubs, for pup wolves often stage mock battles and do a fair amount of snarling and yipping when they feel themselves secure within the confines of their summer range.

By the time I reached the edge of the spruces, the sun was beginning to slide behind them, reminding me that it would soon be time to go home and attend to Paddy's meal, but first I would walk a little way into the trees, continuing to follow a faint game trail that had led me here, on which I found occasional wolf tracks. Fifteen minutes later I discovered something that I had never seen during all my years of traveling through the wilderness—and I have never seen the like of it since, either.

On a narrow, moss- and bush-covered knoll about seventy-five yards long, I found a wolf toilet. The entire knoll was covered with wolf scats and it was easy to see that it had been used by the adults for some time. There were no cub scats, but the adults had just about exhausted all available space. I felt excitement. This place must be close to the summer range and probably to the den where the bitch had given birth to the pups. And I felt surprise. I knew that wolves are fastidiously clean animals, but I had no idea that they actually picked one place on which to deposit their wastes and I had seen no mention of this habit by other observers—and I haven't yet. But perhaps I was jumping to conclusions, I told myself. This, after all, might be the habit of just one pair of wolves who were more fussy than most. Still, I was more inclined to accept the toilet idea as being the rule rather than the exception because it made a great deal of practical sense. Briefly, the habit of wolves is to birth the pups in a den or cave and to keep them there until they are strong enough to travel for short distances; then the bitch usually leads them to a place, such as the spruce forest in which I was walking, where they can run and indulge in mock hunting and begin to learn the facts of lupine life. Biologists call such places rendezvous, and here the pups remain at first, while the adults hunt and bring back food, either carrying it in their mouths or more conveniently storing it in their stomachs and regurgitating it for the pups.

A pack is apt to stay the entire summer in such a rendezvous, even after the pups are old enough to go out on short hunting trips with their parents. Looking now at the plentiful wastes on the knoll, it was reasonable to believe that the adults would adopt such a habit when they were living more or less permanently in one place for the entire summer. If the adults deposited their wastes in the rendezvous, it would quickly get soiled and the cubs would undoubtedly roll in the scats and foul their coats; but perhaps more important, continued soiling in the area of the rendezvous would soon smell up the place, as was made abundantly clear to me while I stood looking at the scats. This could lead to easy discovery of the rendezvous and wolves like to keep as secret as possible the whereabouts of their cubs.

The absence of cub scats, which would have been easily detectable by their smaller size, was not surprising because the pups would be most likely to stay at home and deposit their wastes haphazardly, perhaps even eating them, as young canines are wont to do (sometimes to the horror of pet owners, who think their puppies are filthy), because at that age, rather like human babies, they sample by mouth practically everything that comes their way and sometimes undigested protein passing out with the scats makes these actually appetizing.

Bending down and pulling apart some of the fresher scats with two thin sticks used somewhat like forceps, I noted the bits of bone and hair that they contained and I was once again struck by the formidable constitution of the wolf, which is able to digest and use practically every ounce of protein that it ingests. Indeed, in winter, when hunting is not as easy and when the extreme cold of their northern range puts greater demands upon their systems, wolves void absolutely nothing more than totally indigestible bone chips and fur. Winter scats are quickly recognized. They are conventionally shaped, but they are whitish-gray in color and when examined yield bone and hair bound together with bowel juices and the occasional wisp of sinew, much attenuated, from their victims. By summer these winter scats resemble bleached cattails; if pulled apart then, they fluff out, the compacted fur in each scat, when thus separated, expanding to about an amount equal to a handful.

The first two scats that I examined that afternoon contained unmistakable traces of beaver fur, the third contained a mixture of muskrat fur and porcupine hair and quills, and the fourth and fifth were heavy with the hair of deer. By then I gave up on the sampling, though had I had the time and the equipment, a good survey of the many scats that this place contained would have furnished a detailed and interesting account of the dietary habits of these wolves.

Because it was already late and I was anxious about Paddy, and also because I did not want to hurry my exploration of this place for fear that I might alert the wolves to my presence and cause them to move to another area, I turned back for camp after checking the scats, reaching Alec's Point well after sundown and getting treated to a great display of tantrums from Paddy. He was loud in demanding his Pablum and milk, and he mumbled sulky things under his breath until he had shoved his face into the tin plate.

To make up for my tardiness—and also because I wanted some more blueberries for myself, be it confessed—I took Paddy berry picking again the next morning, making him walk all the way there despite his frequent cries of protest, on the theory that a good walk in the sun would take some of the ginger out of him and he would be more likely to sleep in his lodge for the rest of the day. I wanted to go wolfing right after lunch.

Twelve

Beaver kits are not accustomed to walking long distances in July sunshine, and Paddy, though more conditioned to this kind of activity than other kits of his age because of his practice of following me, was plainly tired when we got back from our trip to Blueberry Flats the next morning. We had set out right after breakfast, at about eight o'clock, and we returned some three hours later. Paddy walked all the way to the Flats and part of the way back, which was more than enough exercise for one small beaver, but in addition he had gamboled in and out of the blueberry bushes and gone on little exploring trips of his own, never getting too far from me, but expending a great amount of energy nevertheless. About a quarter of the way back the kit gave up. He lay down, spread-eagled on the ground, and he would not move another inch. I carried him the remainder of the way home and he fell asleep in my arms.

When I put him over the fence into his nursery he woke up, sat blinking sleepily for a moment or two, looked at me reproachfully—or so my guilt made me believe—and then dived under the water. Soon I heard him scramble into his lodge and scratch around, no doubt finding a comfortable spot on which to sleep. A few minutes later there was silence.

Preparations for my trip to wolf country took only a few minutes. I packed into my "possible bag" one of that morning's cold bannocks, a plastic bag half full of raw oatmeal mixed with raisins, and a canteen of water. I would eat my lunch on the go: half a bannock and two good handfuls of oatmeal and raisins on the way out and the rest of my rations on my way home. Maybe not gourmet fare, this, but definitely sustaining and very easy to prepare and carry and *much* more palatable than the dried beans that the *coureurs de bois* used to munch on in the old days when they pushed their *canots de maître* along the fur-trade routes.

Because I was walking with purpose and not stopping to examine this or that, as is my usual habit, I got to the toilet ridge in about three quarters of an hour. Now I slowed down. I walked as quietly as possible while yet maintaining a casual pace, for nothing spooks wild animals more than the sound of a stealthy tread, which they immediately associate with the approach of a hunter. The time for stalking a wolf, or any other wild animal for that matter, is after you have spotted it and it has not spotted you; then, if conditions are right—such as wind direction and availability of cover—it is frequently possible to approach unobserved. But in my experience, I have found it well near impossible to go in stealth searching for some animal within the shelter of its own range. Animals are cautious and supremely able to interpret sound, and no matter how careful a clumsy, two-footed human may be, it is impossible to creep about the forest without producing all manner of little noises that immediately alert the keen-eared quarry.

Walking normally, on the other hand, often produces good results. This is because animals appear to be able to recognize at least three kinds of foot movement: the hunter's stalk, the unconcealed and purposeful tread of an animal that has sated its appetite and is returning home, and the frantic rush of a scared animal. There are probably other forms of tread that hold meanings for the wild folk, but of these three I am fairly sure.

At one time I used to think that it was impossible to set out with the intention of finding a particular kind of animal within its home range, believing in my ignorance that any sightings I made were purely coincidental—which they were, then, because I had no idea of what I was doing. Later I learned. I discovered that when I was walking quietly but without attempting to conceal my presence, animals did not flee at my coming, sometimes remaining sitting or lying down, at other times standing, alert and in full view, but ready to run if need be and as interested in me as I was in them. Eventually I developed a formula for animal spotting: feel no fear, rid yourself of aggression, remain relaxed, walk easily, use your ears and eyes and nose, and stop often. It works.

That day I deliberately tracked through the wolf toilet, on the theory that the smell of the scats adhering to my boots might overpower my human scent or at least offer some recognizable, safe odor to the noses of the wolves. After that I looked for the signs of travel to this place left when each wolf came here to defecate. I did not, of course, expect a clearly defined trail from rendezvous to toilet, for wolves are much too careful to give themselves away in that fashion and will usually take a different route each time they leave or return to their den or rendezvous; but the wolves had been here many times and I hoped to find some sign that would suggest to me the direction of their summer range.

At first I found lots of signs, but they led me in all directions: old tracks, scuff marks, now and then bits of underfur clinging to tree bark or dead sticks—for this was the time of shedding —here and there faint trails. But all these were dotted around the small ridge like the spokes of a wheel. They offered no directional clue. I kept looking, working my way in circles around the base of the ridge, gradually widening the circumference. It was slow work, but eventually I discovered three faint trails leading toward the northeast. Now I had my guide; rather, I had three of them. Which to follow? Haphazardly I chose the middle one.

Fifteen minutes later I climbed a rise that leveled off suddenly and became a tiny, wedge-shaped plateau. One gnarled and tall white pine grew in the center of the flat, a windswept, branchy tree that must have been a seedling when Astor began trading in furs; the rest of the ground was sparsely covered by mosses, a few ferns, and some low bushes. But beyond the flat, perhaps a quarter of a mile distant, was wolf country, I was sure of it.

It was like a park, that area of forested land that I examined while standing under the big pine, a region of mature pines that because of the shade they cast kept the forest floor clear of lesser growth. Here and there a few seedlings grew, now and then clumps of birch and basswood had found a foothold, but for the most part, the land I could see was carpeted thickly by old pine needles, the kind of forest floor that resists the imprints of running feet. Nevertheless, after some careful searching, I did manage to find an ill-defined trail through the middle of it. Somewhere within the shelter of this forest was the wolf rendezvous I was seeking. Now was the time for caution.

I climbed the old pine tree. Up and up I went, enjoying the feel of the feather-soft needles, and their aroma, and the sound of the small breeze as it moaned gently through the waving lattice of green. Near the crown I found a comfortable perch, and after I pruned away a few small branches that obscured my vision, I sat myself down and had lunch. An hour passed. The land was sleeping its way through the hot time and even the birds were subdued. On the ground, almost a hundred feet beneath my perch, the cicadas rasped their tireless songs and other insects whisked about on erratic journeys, once in a while coming up to visit with me. Once, a big horsefly arrived with hunger in its eye, but before I could splat it with my hat, a swooping hornet grabbed it. Silently I cheered the big, black bug hunter. It took its struggling victim to a sun-drenched branch about three feet from me and there began to eat it. First it trimmed off the wings, one at a time. I watched them drift away. Now the hornet twirled the fly's body with its forelegs, eating as it twirled. In some three minutes, only the ugly head remained and the hornet let this fall. After the meal, the hunter preened its wings, washed its face, and buzzed away.

I sat at ease and feeling most tranquil, almost forgetting my quest as I allowed myself to be mesmerized by the rich and quiet pleasures that surrounded me. Even now as I write about it, I can still smell the scent of pine and I can still feel the cool breeze and hear the chanting cicadas. But all at once my languor was disturbed.

Without any sort of preamble a chorus of high, shrill howls was launched upon the summer air. The wolf pups! I was able to pick out three voices as each cub took its turn to cry wild. But no adult joined the trio. Were the parent wolves away on a hunt? As suddenly as the piping howls began, they ceased and were replaced by some snarling and yapping noises. A yelp, petulant and excited, suggested that one cub had been handled a little too roughly by a brother or sister. Now silence.

I waited expectantly for more sound, estimating that only about half a mile separated me from the cubs and wondering how old they were. Bitch wolves give birth in March, April, May, or early June, depending on their range. In this latitude, late April to early May is the most common whelping time, in which case the pups I had heard would be between two and three months old, capable of accompanying their parents on short hunts, but more likely to stay in the summer nursery while the adults hunted, a task that would now keep them busy, for young wolves grow rapidly and their hunger keeps pace with their increase in size. That was why I was nearly sure that the wolf and bitch were away, foraging in broad daylight when they would probably have preferred to hunt during evening, or at night, when the odds are more in favor of the predator and when there is more movement of the larger prey animals. Wolves, if they are hungry, will hunt at any time of the day or night, of course, but they seem to prefer the hours between sunset and sunrise.

The cubs called again, as suddenly as before. This time they sustained their chorus, yipping at times individually, at other times collectively, an urgent song that made me believe they were calling to their parents. On impulse I cupped my hands around my mouth and howled back, and though I am not very good at imitating a wolf howl, my response set the pups into a veritable paroxysm of howling. I had fooled them. This, I hoped, was my chance to get within sight of them.

I climbed down the tree, circled until the wind was blowing toward me, and began to go forward with as much care as I could muster, now and then stopping to render my poor imitation of a wolf's voice. It worked every time. The pups became more and more excited and after my third call they howled almost continuously for a good five minutes. I was getting close to them by this time and I dared not risk any more imitation calls.

The country through which I now moved was more open and was descending slowly into what appeared to be a fairly large valley in which the pines gave way to spruces and to some deciduous trees and where the ground was liberally covered by a variety of bushes. I moved very slowly, inching along from tree to tree, pausing behind each sheltering trunk to listen and to look and, when I felt that the route was clear, moving forward again, sometimes gaining fifteen or twenty yards, at other times only a few feet. The pups had stopped calling, but occasionally voiced a small snarl or a low growl. They were evidently playing and still unaware of my presence; and they were near.

Because there was no high land from where I could look down into this valley, I began to search for a suitable tree to climb in hopes that I would see the pups from its vantage. It had to be a special tree, tall, but with branches coming down almost to the ground; else, if I attempted to shin up a straight, branchless trunk, the cubs would hear the noise of my body scraping against the bark. I moved even more slowly. The pups howled again; they were no more than two hundred yards from me. I had to find a tree.

As I looked around, an answering howl reached me and the cubs. The deep, ululant voice of an adult wolf seemed to fill the forest. It *had* to be the big wolf; I knew his call by then. Confirming my opinion, a second howl, deep also but less resonant, picked up the first bugle call. That was the bitch. They were close; on the other side of me, but close, and coming quickly. Still I had not found a suitable tree, and if I didn't find one soon, I would lose my chance, for the adults would almost certainly detect me and they would swiftly take their wild children away. For a few moments I debated going back, forgoing this opportunity to see the pups and perhaps the adults in favor of returning another time. I decided against it. I was so very close and in such a good position and I knew that this kind of opportunity does not occur often. I had to find a tree!

I took a chance. Instead of walking slowly and with care, I moved quickly, hoping that the excitement of the pups, which were now yelling in real frenzy, would cover the noise of my passage. And I saw a likely tree. Another pine, younger than the patriarch, only about sixty feet tall, but its limbs came down to within two feet of the ground and formed a veritable stepladder. I climbed, carefully, stopping often to look for the cubs and to listen to their howls. The parent wolves no longer called, but the growing excitement of the young ones suggested that the adults were close.

I was only some thirty feet up the pine when I saw one of the cubs, a little brindled-gray dog thing that was staring intently at the opposite wall of the forest; then, from behind a scrubby spruce tree, the others padded into my sight. One of them was almost identical in color to the first pup, but the third cub was almost black and it had a white star on its chest. All three lined up, sitting on their haunches, turning their heads from side to side and up and down, eager and inquisitive and probably very hungry. They sat in a small clearing, an open space perhaps forty or fifty feet wide by a little more long. All of a sudden they sprang to all fours and dashed forward and almost at the same instant the adults appeared.

I tried to melt my body against the tree trunk. I was sure the wolves would quickly detect me. The pups dashed to their parents and I saw that the adults were not carrying any meat in their mouths. Yipping and whining, the little wolves loped with wagging tails and jumped at their mother and father. The big wolf was in the lead. He stopped, all four legs spread, and he hung his head. The black pup reached him and began to bite at his cheeks and lips, little stimulating nips that would make the adult disgorge some of the meat he carried home in his stomach. The other two pups ran to the bitch; she, too, stopped and, one pup nipping at each side of her face, arched her back, coughed twice, and produced a mass of steaming red meat, which the pups began to eat even before it had cleared her mouth. The black pup, meanwhile, had its mouth inside the cavernous jaws of its father, and by the movements of its head and throat I knew the dog wolf had also regurgitated meat and the pup was eating it as it came up.

Perhaps two minutes the scene lasted. The two with the bitch quarreled and broke away, and the female moved forward, going to stand in the center of the clearing. The male raised his massive head and strolled over to his mate. The three pups scampered behind the adults. Now one of the gray pups got to the big wolf and he arched his back and opened his mouth and disgorged onto the mossy ground. The three pups dived at the red pile. The wolf licked his lips, sniffed at what he had brought up, licked briefly at one of the brindled pups, and lay down a few feet away. His mate joined him and sat on her haunches, watching her feeding young. The male yawned. What a mouth! He flopped onto his side and stretched out full length. He was a monster of a wolf, rawboned and powerful and in top condition. His dark gray coat gleamed like silk, his thick brush of a tail, dark on top and creamy white below, lay straight out, a lavish plume. Beside him, his mate was almost insignificant. She was gray also, but paler and only a little more than half his size. Yet she was not a small wolf. I judged her to weigh between sixty and seventy pounds. Her fur, unlike her mate's, was dull and bare in patches, a usual thing with nursing females of all species at this time of year.

The action had taken place so quickly that until now I had not had time to bring up the field glasses for a better look, though I hardly needed them, for I was only about a hundred yards away from the family. But I wanted to get a really good look at the big wolf, so I lifted the glasses slowly and carefully and focused on the dog. Unsatisfactory. He was lying with his head and neck arched slightly backward and all I could see was the lower part of his jaw and one ear and his closed left eye. I focused on the bitch. She had her back to me. I turned to the pups. Here was action! They were scrambling around, chasing the black one, who was even then swallowing the last morsel of meat.

Moving the arc of my glasses was my undoing. Somehow, I caused a small twig to snap. It was an insignificant noise; anything could have made it, a mouse perhaps, or a bird. But the male wolf was on his feet like a flash and his big yellow eyes looked right up at me. I remained immobile, knowing that most animals are not well able to distinguish form but are incredibly quick at spotting movement. Maybe five seconds passed. The wolf's eyes remained glued on me, and his mate turned and stared also. I stared back, my eyes fixed in their sockets, for I was afraid to swivel my gaze in case the wolves detected even *that* slight movement. I sensed rather than saw the three pups run into hiding, but my gaze was full on the two adults when they turned swiftly and bounded into the spruce forest. For a few heartbeats the sound of their passage endured; then only the cicadas and the birds were left to make music.

This all happened a long time ago, but the scene is as fresh in my memory today as it was during that afternoon in July. I cannot properly express the pleasure and excitement that I felt at seeing the wolves, especially the male. It was more than just a thrilling sight; it was a deep emotional experience, an encounter with the stark, lovely reality of the wilderness that put an indelible mark upon my innermost self.

I climbed down the tree and strolled over to the clearing and examined it with care. Everywhere there were wolf signs.

Bits of gnawed deer bone, strands of wolf fur, chewed sticks and saplings showing where the pups had played, the mosses crushed in many places, scratched up in others. This was the nursery, all right; but would the family return after I had gone? I doubted that they would and I felt regret and I hoped that they would not entirely quit the country. Wolves are touchy about their summer range. They are quick to find a new one if they are disturbed and I most certainly had disturbed them. They might not have been entirely sure of my presence, but they would quickly know if they came back to investigate, which I was sure they would do. My scent could not be disguised from those keen noses; it would tell them that the man thing from the lake had been here.

Walking home, I relived my experience, at one moment feeling again the excitement of the adventure and at the next regretting that I had disturbed the wolf pack. It was not until I knelt beside the campfire and made the pot of tea I so badly wanted that I began to take some measure of satisfaction for having found the rendezvous and actually watched the wolves, even for so short a time. I had in the past seen and studied a number of wolves, but always luck had played the principal part in the sightings. This was different. I had planned to find the summer range and I had done so. I confess to feeling humble satisfaction over the success of my venture.

I was sipping hot tea when Paddy popped up from the water and claimed my attention. He was hungry, he told me in long-suffering mumbles; but he was glad to see me, too, he indicated by rubbing himself against my face. I cuddled the soaking beaver for a few minutes before I put him down and mixed some of his Pablum and milk, noting as I did so that it would soon be time to go out to Mother's store and buy fresh supplies.

When he had fed, Paddy sat at my feet and began one of his lengthy beauty treatments. As I watched him, I was reminded of a European beaver that I saw at Whipsnade Zoo in England. Maybe that Old Country beaver was a little smaller than those found in North America, but there was no other physical difference between the two species. A few years earlier I had read a report on European beaver, which are few in number, and I learned that their common name derives from the old Anglo-Saxon term *beofor* and that these animals, evidently never plentiful in Europe, do not resort to dam and lodge building as a rule but that they can be trained to do so, given the right habitat and conditions. I found this strange at the time and I still do; I wonder whether the European *beofor* originated in the Old World, or whether they migrated to Europe from North America via the Bering land bridge of antiquity.

Popular belief to the contrary notwithstanding, I find nothing strange in the notion that if people and animals could migrate to North America by land, other people and animals could migrate *from* North America to Europe along the same path. What got me thinking along these lines was the *beofor*'s significant failure to build lodges and dams—presumably because it didn't really need to do so in regions where there were rivers and lakes situated in a relatively small land mass (compared to the North American continent). Under those circumstances, the *beofor* would need only to move into a lake or river, dig a bank den, and let it go at that. If my notion is true, in time the Old World clan lost the urge to build the classic structures, but they evidently did not forget *how* to build them. The instinct—if I *must* use the word—remained; they were still programmed. Is it unreasonable, then, to suggest that *beofor*'s ancestors originated in North America? Someday I hope to research this question, and when I do, I shall look for prehistoric clues. Have fossil remains been found in Europe that suggest a side-by-side development of the beaver on both continents at the same time? I do not know of any. On the North American continent, on the other hand, two ancestral beavers were known to exist—the one, as I mentioned earlier, a giant, bear-sized creature which has been named after the state of Ohio, where its petrified bones were first discovered: *Castoroides ohioensis;* the other, smaller (but yet larger than present-day animals), was named *Castor californiensis,* since its more recent remains were found in California.

Today we know of two existent species of beaver, *Castor canadensis,* of North American fame, and *Castor fiber,* of the Old World, though in more recent times *Castor canadensis* also has been transplanted to Europe and Asia and is, by all reports, doing just fine on those continents. This suggests that if the North American animal did *not* migrate to the Old World of its own accord, it undoubtedly could have survived, had it done so.

Paddy returned me to the present when he stood upright and placed his front feet against my leg. He wanted to be held, but I was a little slow in bending forward to pick him up and he didn't wait. Grabbing with his hands at my pants, he hitched up my leg and his back claws dug in through my trousers and left their marks on my skin. I gritted my teeth against the pain and endured, because I was curious to know if he could climb up on his own. He could, with ease, though his tail did not serve him as a prop on the smooth cloth. Here was one more example of the beaver's remarkable construction.

The animal looks ungainly and moves on land in a clumsy manner, but for its own element it has been expertly engineered by nature. Consider its feet: front paws quite hand-like, agile little clutchers that serve it well for carrying mud, rotating sticks, walking on all fours, and scratching itself; its back feet, webbed like a duck's and equipped with long nails, serve two main purposes: they are good paddles and they lend excellent support to the animal when it is climbing, the broad foot covering a wide area and the strong claws able to hook on to the sticks and stones of lodge or dam. Now look at the tail: paddle-shaped, covered with hard, scaly black skin that is more like tanned leather. On land it is an efficient prop when the animal stands upright; in the water it is an aid to steering and diving; on the surface it is a slapping device for emergency identification. It is also a miniature bulldozer. Although the beaver does not consciously use its tail to plaster its lodge or dam, yet the tail does exactly *that*, because it naturally follows behind the animal and, big and wide and heavy as it is, it drags over the wet mud and makes it smooth. On land, it acts in a similar way; at those places where a beaver habitually comes ashore—the animal's slipways—the tail drags over the water-soaked ground and makes it smooth; but it also wears the soil down, in time furnishing the slightly concave pathway so typical of beaver country. Inside the lodge the tail continuously levels the mud floor, smoothing it and the entrance chutes. All this is done by virtue of the fact that the tail follows the beaver, so those who assert that the beaver does *not* use its tail for plastering are correct in that the animal does not *consciously* use it as a tool. But those people who, many years ago, reported that the beaver *does* use its tail for plastering, were also correct.

Those early historians had a keen eye. They noticed that the outsides of newly plastered lodges were smooth and they noticed the smooth slipways; they noticed, too, the beaver's small hands, quite useless as trowels, and they looked at the broad, oval tail, and even though they had never seen a beaver using this for plastering, they concluded that the only way the animal could make smooth the walls of its lodge was by using its tail. And they were quite right; the myth and the fact are related. It is only a matter of interpretation: the tail is a useful but *involuntary* trowel.

The beaver's tail has yet another purpose, however. It is a storage place for fat, which, according to most authorities, the animal uses up during the lean months of winter. I agree and disagree with this theory. Yes, the beaver uses up its fat reserves during winter, as all wild animals do, but these "emergency rations" are drawn from all parts of its body, including the tail. This is not the only reason for the fat; it is not even the principal reason.

Logic suggests the correct answer. The fat in a beaver's tail serves as antifreeze. Examine the tail closely: it is hairless except for a few bristles; thus it is very much exposed to the weather and in winter would freeze solid and break off if it were not for its content of fat. *That* is the principal reason for the large amount of fat in a beaver's tail, a characteristic shared in lesser measure by the muskrat, who also possesses a hairless tail and who also stores extra fat in this appendage to protect it against subzero cold. The tough, outward skin of the tails of both these animals is almost impervious to destruction, but the tailbone and the muscles and nerves inside the appendage must be insulated against the cold.

It was early evening; a July thunderstorm raged through the bushland. It started with some frowning sky, high humidity, swarms of mosquitoes, and finally, when the heavens really became angry, the first spear of lightning was flung to earth and the first giant clap of thunder shook the very ground. There had been other storms since I arrived at Old Alec's Lake, but this was the first really good one, and Paddy, who had been sitting beside me in the open doorway of the tent, almost turned himself inside out as he fled to my sleeping bag, where, in his panic to tunnel under it, he emptied his bowels.

Never again will I say that beavers cannot move fast! Paddy, I am sure, beat all castorian records in quitting the tent doorway, reaching my sleeping bag, defecating, and diving under the covers.

I went to him and put one hand inside the bedroll and stroked him and talked to him. In a few minutes he calmed, but he refused to come out and I left him and cleaned his mess off my bed. Just as I finished, another cataclysmic roar escaped from the heavens and Paddy burrowed deeper into the bag. "My God, no!" I said out loud, thinking the second thunderclap might have produced another mess. I unzippered the bag and revealed a cringing Paddy, but no scats. I picked him up and cuddled him, telling him to stay calm, but the lightning and its companion bangs had increased and Paddy kept shaking.

I knew that beaver generally avoid the rain, remaining in their lodges during a storm, but I had supposed that they did so because the noise of thunder and of falling rain increased the chances of a stalking predator. Now I wondered. Paddy's fear was as real as it was unusual in a wild animal, even a young one, all of which do not seem to be overly concerned by the sound of thunder. I pondered the matter, but I could find no logic in the kit's fear. In any case, the idiosyncrasies of one beaver did not mean that all of them shared the trait. Inasmuch as I have not had any further opportunity to study the effect of thunder on beaver populations, I am still unable to say whether the clan as a whole dislikes thunder for some obscure reason, or whether Paddy was an exception.

I put my beaver child back to bed, covered him over, and piled an extra blanket over the top of him, insulating him in some measure from the din that was continuing outside. After that, I dragged my folding campstool back to its place in the tent doorway—I had kicked over the little seat when I rose to comfort Paddy—and I indulged myself storm watching. I am always fascinated by a good summer thunderstorm. The fat lightning angling down, the black clouds, the big winds, the giant thunderclaps, and the rain, the deluge, fanned by the wind, hitting the tent and turning my shelter into a drum. . . . I sat and I looked and I listened and felt warm and comfortable and secure.

Thirteen

It was still raining the next day. The pattering of drops on the tent awoke me at first light of a gray and sullen morning, but when I got up and unzippered the doorway, I saw that last night's downpour had been replaced by a fine, steady rain that looked as though it was going to continue for another twenty-four hours. This was a nuisance; I needed supplies and had intended to go out and get them today, but I wasn't keen to undertake the eight-hour round trip in wet weather; on the other hand, the rain was a comfort, coming at a time when the country had become tinder dry and unbearably hot. I had been worrying about forest fires, three of which I had experienced in the past; they had left me with an indelible memory of the most fearful and formidable force to be found in nature.

Turning from the tent doorway, I noted the lump at the foot of my sleeping bag made by Paddy's gently snoring bulk. I was reminded of the restless night that the kit had spent and I envied his ability to relax now so completely; I too was tired, for he had kept me awake, but instead of being able to sleep away the night's tensions as he was doing, I was wide awake and irritable, wanting my breakfast, but not wanting to go outside to get my packsack from where it was suspended on the pine tree.

I am one of those contradictory types that can be infinitely patient in some things and intolerantly impatient in others, a schism that often clashes with a nature that is habitually tidy and insists that its belongings be orderly, yet rebels at performing some of the chores necessary for securing this order. Even under normal conditions I was mildly irked by the task of continually raising and lowering my food packs from the tree branch, but this morning I was actually annoyed by the need to do so and I was again reminded that I had not constructed a proper food cache, as I had planned. Because of the mood I was in, I blamed Paddy for my own shortcomings, telling myself that I had been too busy taking care of the kit to build the cache. By the time a half hour had elapsed, I managed to fan myself into an ugly frame of mind that was hardly mitigated after I got the packsack and prepared a dismal breakfast of boiled oatmeal sweetened with blueberries and washed down with weak coffee.

My food was really very low. I had enough coffee for two days if I made it weak, enough flour for two lots of bannock, one can of corned beef, and one can of beans; there was sufficient powdered milk and Pablum for two feeds for Paddy, and about one pound of dried beans and some tea. Tomorrow I would have to go to Mother's, rain or shine.

As I sat glowering, Paddy woke up and crawled out of the bag, a dopey, slow-moving beaver that sniffed halfheartedly at the pan where the remains of my oatmeal were solidifying into a gel, hesitated as though to taste the stuff, and then came directly to me, standing on his hind legs and asking to be picked up for a cuddle. The kit's simple, affectionate gesture made me ashamed of my nasty temper. I smiled, picked him up, and gave myself a stern lecture as I held him against my neck and stroked his head. Five minutes later I had regained my normal mood and I took Paddy to his nursery, where he wasted no time in submerging and entering his lodge.

Paddy had been weaned, theoretically, though I still gave him one feed of formula in the evenings. In the wild, beaver kits begin to eat green food within a few days of birth, but they nurse until they are between two and two and a half months old. Paddy, raised on a diet that was much richer than his mother's milk, had been slow to start eating plants, but by now he fed on any green food that took his fancy, even managing to cut down a few small saplings, and this, I felt, was something of a feat because it has been fairly well established that beaver must learn to cut down trees by watching their parents.

Six days before the rainstorm I had more or less parted Paddy from Pablum and milk after he had spent an entire afternoon and most of the evening eating in his nursery while I watched from a distance, trying to observe his every movement. Just before my suppertime I remarked to myself that he obviously no longer needed the formula, but as though he had read my thoughts, he turned from munching some poplar leaves and waddled up to the fence, nosing it and mumbling a couple of times to attract my attention.

I had gone and lifted him out, cuddled him for a few moments, and set him down beside the fireplace, whereupon he called for his Pablum and milk. I ignored him, beginning preparations for my evening meal, and he was patient for a time, content to sit and watch as I fried a nice bass that I had caught that morning near Bass Island. It was a big fish that had taken the little yellow spoon in classic fashion, striking just as the lure hit the water.

Watching the fish sizzle in the pan and sniffing the delicious aroma it was releasing sharpened my hunger and made me forget about Paddy. I began debating about what part of the fish I would eat for supper and what part I would save for breakfast, examining the matter seriously, for such things become important when gustatorial pleasures are few. The greedy side of me wanted to cut the fish in half across the body and eat the tail part tonight—the tastier and more bone-free —while the more provident side of my nature advised slicing the fish lengthways and eating half of the body at each meal, the good with the not so good. I had not yet resolved this dilemma when Paddy clawed his way onto my lap and pushed his damp face against my neck, clearly asking for his formula. I couldn't resist his appeal! I mixed a smaller amount of Pablum and milk and gave it to him, and he was satisfied and content to return to his pen when he had finished eating. From then on I gave him a token feed once a day, usually in the evening, for he was now spending his nights eating or playing in his nursery and his days sleeping in his lodge, from where he emerged in late afternoon to greet me before beginning to nibble on plants.

Last night, because of the thunderstorm, the kit had elected to stay in the tent, but normally he preferred to live outside, where he was often visited by some of the other beaver, whose tracks I would find every morning at various places beside the wire fence. The large marks left by the buck were the most conspicuous and numerous, and looking at these tracks every day, it was clear that the buck and at least one of the older kits were regular visitors during the night, though the adult beaver that I thought to be a young female came only occasionally. And I was sure that Paddy no longer feared the others. Wherever their tracks showed outside the wire I would find his tracks inside the fence, suggesting that there was regular communication between the kit and the others.

After Paddy disappeared into his lodge on that rainy morning, I decided that it was just about time to take the fence down and allow him full freedom, and I resolved to do so the next day, when I returned from my shopping trip, though I was still somewhat worried about his safety; I could not be totally certain that the other beaver would accept him in the colony. I remember that I sat in the tent for a good two hours pondering the matter and at last concluded that Paddy would have to face the risk sooner or later if he was to live wild after I left this place. It seemed to me that the younger he was, the better would be his chances of acceptance, because the others would be less likely to see a threat in him at this age.

By the time I finished debating this matter I had become restless by the unusually long period of inactivity and I was glad to see that the clouds were thinning under the influence of a brisk southwest wind. Sometime past noon the drizzle changed to sporadic showers, then stopped altogether; a lone spear of sunlight brightened the far side of the lake, the mist began to clear. The wind playing through the treetops and the drip-drip-drip of water slipping off the branches and leaves was the only sound in a wilderness gone suddenly quiet, until a squirrel shrilled and a flock of blue jays moved into the area of the campsite and made raucous the day with their effervescent voices. Slow-moving white clouds sailed in from the south and pushed the gray out of the sky; the sun emerged.

I went outside, climbed Spring Rock, and looked around with the field glasses, noting at once that the three beaver dams were almost covered by water. Only the top sticks and the alders and other bushes growing on the dams were visible, showing that the lake level had risen considerably. For a few minutes I watched and listened to the waters pouring out of East Creek and I wondered what had happened at the other two ponds, particularly West Pond, which was fed by the waters escaping from East Pond. I would go and see.

I hadn't yet had lunch, so I packed some oatmeal and blueberries and took along a canteen of water and the field glasses. Soon I found myself walking through a country swollen with moisture: Deer Valley was almost a stream, Blueberry Flats squelched underfoot, there were little pools of water all over the landscape. We had needed rain, but it seemed that nature had overdone it somewhat.

I reached the high ground that overlooks the northern ponds in about three quarters of an hour and by then I was soaked from the waist down by the water that clung to the bushes and tree branches. The mosquitoes were in top form, thirsting for my blood, a pursuing cloud of mites that made life difficult every time I stopped to scan the country through the glasses. I had my little bottle of repellent, of course, but the insects were so numerous and persistent that they managed to find many places unprotected by OFF!, and had I not been so curious about the water level of the two ponds, I believe I would have turned back and waited for the sun to dry the country and cause the horde of pests to seek shelter from the heat on the undersides of leaves and grass stems.

When I saw the ponds I was unprepared for the sight that met my gaze, even though I had half supposed that they would be flooded. The small neck of swamp that connected them no longer existed, the two ponds were now one; the dam on West Pond had been partly washed out by the flash flood, roiling water poured out of the break in a noisy journey westward, creating a low rumble that dominated all other sounds. Presently I saw movement near the dam. I raised the glasses. Three beaver had emerged on the surface, two adults and one young one; all carried sticks and were swimming toward the breach, intent on repairing the damage. A few seconds later four more young ones appeared from behind the lodge, swimming in line astern. The colony had turned out in defense of its water supply.

The five young ones, all about Paddy's size, were actively helping their parents to carry sticks and branches to the dam, wedging them into the break as neatly as the adults were doing. I had seen this sort of thing many times before and I knew what the routine would be, but I watched, sitting as comfortably as possible on a wet rock, my elbows propped on my knees to steady the glasses.

As a rule, I knew, the adult beaver in a colony look after dam repairs, but in emergencies the entire family turns out and everybody pitches in to stem the escape of water. The young are not able to equal the work of the adults, but they literally pull their weight in branches and pond debris, copying the actions of their parents, in this way receiving practical instruction in dam building.

Much has been written about the building and repairing of dams, and some rather ridiculous claims have been made about the beaver's abilities, all of which appear to hinge upon the opinion that each writer has of the animal's level of intelligence. When the first Europeans arrived on the American continent, they quickly learned to trap beaver for its fur and for its meat, which became an important part of their diet, and in consequence they held the beaver in high regard. Many of the writings of the early settlers that I had read suggested that they were awed by *Castor's* amazing skills and that they believed the animal possessed almost human intellect, opinions that were no doubt influenced by Indian legends that often endowed the big rodent with supernatural powers.

Today, as I write this narrative, biologists have dispelled those early fantasies, but while doing so, many of them have swung the pendulum to the opposite extreme, belittling the beaver's intelligence and even going so far as to say that the animal is actually stupid. By human standards the beaver is not a genius (it doesn't *need* to be); nevertheless, the rodent is not the dolt that some would have it to be. Such observers suggest that the animal is little more than a programmed machine, and they attempt to support their views by claiming that the beaver often selects the wrong sites for its dams when better locations are available nearby; they also insist that beaver build dams and lodges purely by instinct and thus cannot be rated as intelligent mammals.

However this may be, my own experiences with beaver have convinced me that this animal has far *more* intelligence than it is being given credit for and far *less* than it was credited with by the early settlers. But how can one measure this level of intellect by human standards? I do not believe this can be done with any degree of success; not, at any rate, by using present experimental methods. Instead I prefer to examine the beaver's many accomplishments as I have observed them in the wild—in the *natural* environment of this animal—then base my conclusions on my findings.

Before I rescued Paddy, I was already convinced that beaver have better-than-average intelligence when their capabilities are measured by the standards of other wild animals; my relationship with the kit and the other beaver of the colony simply confirmed this conviction. Paddy learned easily; young as he was when I found him, it took him no time at all to associate his personal comfort and safety with my presence, sound, touch, and scent. He had never before come into contact with man and had obviously never heard human speech, but within hours he could associate my voice with his needs;

he showed that he was able to reason when he discovered the unusual comfort of the sleeping bag and determined to occupy it in preference to his natural resting place, the bare floor; within two days he learned that the noise made by the zipper when I opened the tent doorway was harmless, while he continued to remember the hunting whistle of the hawk. Again and again Paddy showed that he was intelligent, alert, and capable of forming simple judgments.

I suppose that a behavioral psychologist would have taken Paddy and subjected him to a variety of tests and then compared the results with similar tests undergone by a dog or a horse. Such tests have actually been conducted; they purport to show that beaver are 50 percent less intelligent than dogs. Well, I'll buy that when I find a dog that is able to build a beaver dam!

At any rate, when I am asked—as I often am—if a beaver is intelligent, I have no hesitation in answering in the affirmative, but I do not attempt to compare its intelligence with that of a dog or a horse because I cannot see any real basis for comparison between domestic and wild animals. The horse and the dog are hybrids, creatures whose evolution has been altered by man's genetic tinkering, as a result of which they have become pretty much dependent upon man for their survival. Like Tommy Tucker, these animals have learned to sing for their supper after thousands of years of domestication; they belong to the world of man, and if they are exposed to the tests and rewards of behaviorists, they find nothing too unusual in the game and they are often able to "do the right thing" because they have become amazingly adept at reading their human masters. In other words, they are not being challenged by forces that are completely outside of their natural environment.

But how different it is for a wild animal, even one that has been born in captivity, to find itself faced by a variety of mechanical contrivances in the garish sterility of a laboratory! I would not expect such an animal to function effectively.

It is interesting to note that the beaver became the world's first engineer when it learned to construct and control its own environment, and it was almost certainly the first mammal to build a solid dwelling for itself. While the early hominids were still reduced to living in whatever accidental shelters they could find, the beaver was living in warm, secure homes and installing dams to keep a good depth of water in its "castle moat." Maybe they *are* programmed by instinct today, but somewhere in the mists of prehistory, there was at least one super-intelligent beaver that figured out techniques of lodge and dam construction and passed them on to its descendants.

How do beaver build dams? It all depends on the country, the current, the body of water, the available materials, and probably a good number of other things. The most quoted method is as follows: A beaver first selects the place where the dam is to go; next it begins to gather sticks and poles, taking them one at a time to the dam site, grasping them with its teeth and towing them, much as it does when it is gathering materials for its lodge. If the stick is large and the current strong, the swimming animal must hold its tail at a slant to the direction in which it wants to travel to compensate for the flow of current against its burden. At the dam site the beaver wedges its stick and goes to get another one and so on until it has bridged the gap.

As I said, this is the most quoted explanation of dam building. It is all right as far as it goes; but it does not go far enough. To fully explain dam construction, it is first necessary to examine the *kinds* of dams that beaver build and the kinds of *locations* where they are placed. For the sake of clarity, let us view these things from the standpoint of a beaver that has been ejected from its home colony because of overpopulation.

If the outcast is lucky, it may find a suitable river or lake in which to live and it will not need to build a dam at all. But if it cannot find a ready-made water reservoir not already occupied by other beaver, it must make its own pond, either by using runoff from an established beaver pond or by damming a small stream or creek. In any event, the prime necessity when building a pond from scratch is a supply of water. This does not need to be large, but it must be fairly constant in order to fill up depressed land contours to the required depth of four or five feet, at a minimum, so that the water will not freeze to the bottom.

Starting from dry land, the beaver has little difficulty making dams; it simply drags brush and debris to the sites and piles them up. As the water rises and finds its way through the cracks and holes of the barricade, the beaver wedges in more sticks, stones, mud, plants, or whatever is handy, until the escaping water slows down to a trickle. In a short time, leaves and other bits of debris carried by the current are caught by the new dam, helping to retain more water. If the incoming water supply is good, the level of the new pond rises steadily and quickly; if the supply is poor, the level is slow to rise and the beaver then depends on rain to help bring the water to the required depth.

When the new pond is a large one and the water rises well, the beaver must raise the height of its dam and broaden the base. In time, the dam reaches the proper height and from that point on the beaver limits itself to making periodic repairs as needed.

In building its dams, the beaver uses a definite technique, placing the sticks it carries on the *downface* side of the dam location and setting them side by side so that each stick or pole presents the least amount of surface to the flow of water; between each stick, the beaver wedges mud, plants, or stones. In a very general sort of way, beaver use sticks and mud much as a bricklayer uses bricks and mortar, except that the animals start wide at the base and narrow the wall as it rises. The length of each stick or pole varies from about two feet to as many as six, sometimes even longer, and as a rule the long sticks form the base of the dam and the shorter ones are used higher up. This is not always the case, however, especially on an old dam which is almost continually being strengthened or repaired. Such dams look ragged and it is hard to visualize any order in their construction, but they are firmly based and for this reason there is no longer any need to be precise in placing a pole or stick on their lips. Often, overflowing water moves the top sticks and invariably ground vegetation takes root on the larger dams and helps to keep them together.

Let us now suppose that the outcast beaver is lucky and finds a shallow pond or creek suitable to its needs. In this case, the pond must be deepened and the animal chooses a dam site (or more than one, if need be) and begins to work underwater, forming a base out of mud and stones. On this base it packs sticks and poles, which are either wedged into the debris, weighted down by stones, or are already waterlogged and thus remain on the bottom. When the base begins to rise out of the surface, the beaver drags up more sticks and laces them in, finishing the dam as already described, in this way enlarging the reservoir.

Some ponds may need only one dam, others may have four or five; often one pond leads to another when new arrivals take advantage of the original pond's runoff and build dams to retain the escaping water for their use, much as the beaver of West Pond did, using the water that ran out of East Pond.

How long are beaver dams? Anywhere from three or four feet to the longest recorded, which measured 2,140 feet and was located on the Jefferson River, near Three Forks, Montana. If there is such a thing as an "average" dam, it will probably measure about twenty feet in length and will curve toward the downstream side. But because there are always so many variables in terrain and, presumably, in the personalities of the dam builders, no one dam is like another. Some curve at an angle, others are straight, others may zigzag repeatedly, depending on whether the beaver was avoiding obstacles when he built the dam, or whether the animal wanted to take advantage of a tree or a rock to help anchor its structure, or whether the current was strong enough to give the builder problems, breaking the initial wall of sticks so that it swung out at various places.

I have seen little dams, maybe only a couple of feet high and some three feet wide at the base, that because they had been placed atop a natural rise of land held back as much water as a dam five or six feet high on the downface side, though some dams may reach a height of ten or twelve feet at the center and have a base twelve to twenty feet wide. In my experience, all dams are solid enough to allow foot travel over them; some are even wide enough and strong enough to take the weight of a team of horses.

Sometimes beaver pull out a dam if it suits their needs, particularly on rivers during summer conditions if rain is scarce. The river near which my wife and I own a retreat is a good example of this. In the time that I have known it, I have found constant changes in dam location on the Gibson River. This is because there is one old colony about four miles upriver that has built a high, long, wide dam and has created a veritable lake behind it. This dominant colony controls the water level of the river, and the lesser colonies downstream must make do with what water spills over or escapes the big dam. The thing works on a sort of progression basis: the beaver nearest to the big dam get first crack at the overflow, and if there is not enough of it to maintain a proper depth over the entire length of that part of the river that they have chosen for their home reservoir, they build a new dam farther upriver, abandoning the original barrier and in this way reducing the size of their "pond" but increasing the depth of water.

When the next colony downstream becomes aware of this development, its members will swim upstream and take apart the abandoned dam, thus allowing the second lot of runoff to swell their part of the river, while the last colony, the "poor relations" of beaver country, must make do with whatever escapes the second dam: they too make smaller their part of the river by building a new dam closer to the outflow of the second colony. But if heavy rains come, or during the spring flood, the master builders upriver usually breach a hole in their dam to let out the water so that their lodges do not become flooded. When this happens, the lesser ones quickly take advantage of the spill-off by building new dams downstream and enlarging their water boundaries. Making a canoe trip up the Gibson River is always something of an adventure; one just does not know what to expect at the next bend.

Some biologists contend that beaver can be induced to build dams anywhere by playing to them a tape recording of rippling water—this is taken as further evidence that dam building is purely instinctive—but this claim is hardly convincing, because, as anyone who has spent time near a beaver dam will know, water is *continuously* trickling through the dam and the sound of it does not in any way send the beaver into a frenzy of dam building. Moreover, beaver who live in lakes and large rivers where they are assured of a continuous supply of deep water, do not build dams at all, and no amount of rippling-water tape recordings will be likely to make them do so. How, then, did this claim come about? I fear that someone has used captive beaver as experimental subjects and has played the tape to them and has concluded from the response obtained that all beaver are thus stimulated into dam building. If this is how the contention got started—and I confess I don't know, but this seems the only way to impel beaver to listen to a tape recorder—it once again points out the futility of studying animals in captivity.

All captive wild animals suffer from frustration, and just as imprisoned raccoons wash their food "for something to do," perhaps captive beaver, bored and listless in their purposeless confinement, could be induced to build dams to the sound of rippling water on a tape. This, in my view, would only go to prove that some very aberrant habits get started among zoo animals, as they do among the inmates of human prisons.

Apart from building dams and lodges, beaver also dig canals in some areas of their range to enable them to go in safety farther from the home pond to cut down food trees. In some cases these canals are only shallow slipways a few yards long, but in many instances they are 200 and 300 feet long (the longest recorded, in Michigan, I believe, stretched for 745 feet). Digging these canals would not appear to pose problems for such expert burrowers, until one realizes that if one canal is not able to reach a desirable stand of trees because the terrain slopes up from the pond, the beaver builds its channels in steps, creating "locks." In this way, the lower canal is filled by lake or pond water and the higher levels are filled from ground seepage, runoff, or springs. Strangely, this part of the beaver's industry is often omitted from the literature, yet construction of the stepped canals is more difficult and demands greater experience than the building of a lodge or dam.

Sometimes beaver build little side ponds adjacent to their homes so as to have safe access to choice feeding areas. There is one such on the Gibson River that my wife and I explored one spring; it is located at a point of the river where an eighty-foot rock scarp rises sheer from the shoreline. Whenever we canoed past this cliff, we heard water falling, but we could not see where it was coming from because of dense shoreline vegetation. One day I nosed the canoe into the bank and we got

out and pushed through the underbrush to find a small dam—
about nine feet long and only a couple of feet high—blocking
a little channel that had been formed by water that was falling
from above.

It wasn't exactly a waterfall, rather a broad seepage, so that
water came down from a dozen or more places. We climbed
the rock to find an area of dense forest growing atop a
plateau, through the center of which a wide creek flowed and
leaked over the rocks to feed the river below. I did not trace
the source of this water, so I cannot say whether it was simply
ground seepage caused by the thaw or whether it originated in
a spring up there. One day I have promised myself to find out,
when I have time.

In this case the beaver has built the dam to stop the cliff
runoff from escaping into the river, and the result is a nice,
fairly deep pool, snug against the rock face, surrounded by
succulent foodstuff, including quite a good number of poplars.
Here, in summer, the beaver can feed on tender ground vegetation that they are not able to find on the riverbanks, and
they feed secure in the knowledge that they can quickly dive
into their small pool if they are disturbed.

I have seen many other such side ponds, some taking advantage of similar spring or runoff conditions, others just
small and narrow extensions of the main pond, little basins
dammed at several places to provide safe access to food. The
smallest and most inland of these that I have ever seen was
built almost two miles from the main pond in an area of Ontario where Cambrian granite forms a series of small ridges
and valleys. The animals had dug canals from their pond
through one of the valleys and had gradually extended their
feeding range far from the home pond. One adventurous animal had gone even further. The beaver had to dig a long,
curved canal around one ridge in order to bring water to a
depression that was about fifteen feet wide by thirty feet long

on the south side of which grew a thick stand of white poplar.

I was walking through this part of the bush one afternoon in spring when I was truly startled by a tail slap that seemed to be coming from the middle of a dry forest. When I checked, I discovered the tiny pond, its waters muddied by the beaver's dive. I found myself a seat and waited. Within about five minutes up came the pond builder, sniffing and flicking its ears and quite nervous, presumably because it had been caught a long way from home. I remained still and the beaver did not detect me. After it had checked the area, it evidently decided that it would return home. Carefully it steered itself to the canal entrance and I watched it swim into the next valley pond.

On the afternoon that I watched the beaver in West Pond repair the damage to their dam, I was not preoccupied with questions about their intellect or about whether or not they had acquired their skills instinctively or by learning; I was too busy trying to observe them all, plotting their actions as they worked to stem the flow of water. But the two hours that I spent observing them through the glasses led me to form two conclusions, both of which I noted in my book at the time:

"Beaver show variations in IQ, rather like people. The kits do not all work in the same way, neither do they all have the same skill. One is definitely clumsy; it loses more sticks than it manages to wedge in the dam—it is the smallest of the five. The brightest is the one I first saw with parents; it stays with one or other of adults and seem to copy all their actions—a fast learner.

"All the kits are learning as they work. They are improving techniques as they work. Sometimes adults help wedge loose sticks, especially when 'Dopey' brings them."

These were elementary notes, of course, and I found little significance in them at the time because in those days I took it for granted that any animal in possession of a cortex had the ability to think and to reason within the limits of its brain development, just as I took it for granted that there would be variations in IQ among members of the same species. I was not aware then that the beaver was thought by some biologists to be stupid and instinctive, or I would probably have watched that family for a longer time.

Fourteen

Mother peered at me intently, her faded eyes twinkling behind her granny glasses; she hesitated, then blurted out the question that must have been dying to come out ever since the first time that I bought Pablum and the feeding bottle at her store.

"And why would you be needing baby food to study beaver, young man?"

It was the day after I had watched the West Pond beaver repair their dam, and I was once again buying supplies after a relatively fast canoe trip in a country that was swollen with rainwater. I had been able to take shortcuts that allowed me to shave almost an hour off my normal time.

Answering Mother's questions, I told her all about Paddy, and for a time we discussed beaver and the country, though I was deliberately vague about the location of Old Alec's Lake; I didn't want gossip to bring it to the notice of some local trapper who might decide to stake a claim on the forgotten region.

After our chat, Mother remained behind her counter, leaning on it, while I picked the rest of my purchases off her shelves, piling the goods beside her hand-operated cash register. When I was finished she totaled my bill in silence; then she turned to me, holding on to the slip of paper as though she wanted to delay my departure. I knew I was going to be treated to a story.

"My Alfred trapped beavers hereabouts," Mother began, looking down at the bill in her hands. "Forty-some years ago, it was. I used to go with him and look after the cabin and cook and I used to help him flesh the blankets. They was good days, too."

Mother stopped, a faraway look in her eyes. I could not imagine this frail little lady busy with the chore of fleshing a stretched beaver blanket.

"But then he went and fell through the ice. One January, it was. He was coming back with four beavers and he took a shortcut across this pond and the ice had heaved and he fell through. He was nigh frozen to death when he got back to our cabin and he'd lost the beavers in the pond. Well, he took *pneumony* and us twelve mile in the bush and not a soul around to run to for help."

Again she paused, a little smile on her lips. She was happy with her reminiscences, that was obvious, though I couldn't understand why Alfred's accident and illness should bring a smile to her face.

She told me that he became too ill to walk and that she had been unable to go out for help through more than four feet of snow, "us only having snowshoes." What did she do? I asked.

"I nursed him, that's what. Blackstrap molasses and brown paper and turpentine and lots of blankets. And I pounded him on the back five times a day and twice at night and made him cough up the flux. And, you know, he got well. But I set down my foot after that. 'No more trapping, Alfred,' I said to him. We'd been married five years and I'd taken care of the cash money because my Alfred, he was a free spender, especially at fur-selling time, when we went to town, and after he sold all our furs he'd go with the boys to the tavern and they'd have themselves quite a time while I was shopping. First time it happened my Alfred spent almost half the fur money.

"After that I'd go with him to the auction and I'd take care of the money and give him some, so he could have a beer with the boys and maybe treat them a round, but no more. It was too hard to come by that beaver money. Catching beavers is surely hard work."

I nodded, but didn't speak. She had more to tell me and I wanted to hear it all.

"Oh my, but my Alfred, he was sure dead set against giving up trapping! He said to me, he did: 'What else can a man do hereabouts?' That's when I told him. You see, for the last two years this store had been up for sale. It wasn't much of a place, mind you, but the owner only was asking eight hundred dollars cash money and another three hundred for the stock. Well, I had almost two thousand dollars saved, fur money, all of it, but Alfred didn't know I had that much."

Mother and Alfred bought the store, which was just as well, for the trapper not only got pneumonia when he fell through the ice, he also lost two toes off his right foot and three off his left through frostbite.

"But he wasn't altogether a cripple, you know? He could

hobble around and do chores and two years later he applied to be postmaster when the mail came through here. *He* had to apply because they wouldn't give it to a woman, you know? But really *I* was the postmaster, because my Alfred was never good with figures."

Mother paused once more; then she looked me in the eyes and smiled.

"Beavers are good animals, young man. They sure are! I wouldn't have this store, but for beavers."

Mother gave me the bill. I settled the account and we chatted for a few more minutes. When I left, my thoughts were centered on the little lady's story; its theme was familiar to me, even though the details differed. It was the story of trapping as it used to be when men (and their women) all over North America pursued the elusive fur of *Castor* while forever hoping that one year the catches would be large and the price of fur would climb high, a dream that seldom came true, but which was enough for those hardy people, who found in their wild, free life a kind of satisfaction seldom encountered in the more prosaic and restrictive endeavors so common today.

I too had fallen under the spell when Old Alec's often-repeated stories fired my imagination and, short as my experience was, I count myself fortunate today to have had the opportunity at a time when trapping techniques were still pretty much the same as they had been in the earliest days of the fur trade. How different it is today! A modern trapper rides over his trapline on a fast motor toboggan, covering in a day a route that used to take me two weeks to complete on snowshoes; and because of the snow machine such a trapper is able to bring his catch back so that the tedious task of skinning can be done in the comfort of a warm room instead of on top of the snow in temperatures that often plunge well below freezing.

Even the traps are improved nowadays, the old leg-hold devices being largely replaced by the modern Connibears, which work more effectively and kill instantly—this, of course, is also a much more humane way of taking fur. Like the old traps, snowshoes, and dog teams, the line cabin is also a thing of the past; it is no longer needed unless the trapline is very long.

The last time I went trapping was in 1968, for one day, with a neighbor who ran a line near my property. We left at eight o'clock in the morning and we were back at home before dark, having covered some fifty miles by snowmobile. I could not help recalling the last days on my own trapline in the Lake of the Woods, remembering particularly the long, cold walk that I was faced with one evening, carrying almost ninety pounds on my back because I needed the meat of the two beaver that I had caught. I had left my line cabin at six o'clock in the morning in temperatures that had dropped to 20 degrees below zero.

I had put out twenty-eight sets that were widely scattered over the line, and the first one I visited yielded a beaver that weighed about forty pounds; I shouldered the dripping burden and spent the rest of the day checking the other traps. By afternoon, the beaver I was carrying had frozen, and when I lifted a second animal from a set I gave up for the day.

I was about ten miles from the line shack by this time, and although I could have made a fire and skinned the freshly cut beaver while waiting for the other to thaw, the lateness of the hour and my need for a meal decided me to carry both of them back to the cabin.

It was almost ten o'clock at night when I reached my shelter, exhausted and nearly frozen, and ravenous, but before I could eat I had to kindle a fire in the old tin heater. By the time I had got warm and had supper and had skinned the two beaver, it was after midnight, and I turned in with the knowl-

edge that I must rise at first light next day and snowshoe another eight miles home, carrying the fur and the meat on my
back, the beaver blood soaking through the packsack and my
clothes. I received thirty-five dollars for those two beaver
blankets.

That trip astride Aut Adams's snowmobile, zipping easily
through the frozen wilderness, made me realize that I had
lived through the end of an era, and afterward, while we sat in
Aut's white bungalow and talked about trapping, he surprised
me by voicing regrets for the old way. Sure, he said, it was
faster, easier, and more convenient to cover the trapline by
snowmobile, but he missed walking through the country, seeing things, stopping to watch a bird or an animal, and having
"all the time in the world to think." Trapping was just a business now, he said; he made more money because he could
cover more territory and this was good for him and his family,
but he didn't like it as well. Neither did I.

The major difference between the old way and the new way
of trapping is the speed of travel, which somehow makes the
occupation much less personal; just as fast automobiles and
superhighways put the scenery out of reach of driver and pas-
sengers, so do snowmobiles prevent the wilderness traveler
from observing the more intimate details of nature.

I am certain that I would have learned precious little about
the beaver and its country had I stinkpotted my way over my
trapline riding a noisy motor toboggan, just as I am certain
that I would have no part of such a vehicle were I again to
follow a trapline today, regardless of the practical advantages.
You know, I have a feeling that I might, over a period of time,
wind up dollars ahead by using snowshoes on the job! I still
own the snowshoes that I used to walk my line in the Lake of
the Woods: they cost me thirteen dollars when I bought them
and they are good for a lot more years of tramping. The last
time I spoke to another trapper of my acquaintance, he had

managed to go through three snowmobiles in five years: the first one cost him $700, the second cost him $900 and his old machine as a trade-in, and the third one set him back $1,200. One must work hard to get $2,800 worth of furs just to pay for transportation. But apart from the economics of the issue, and regardless of them, I would never use a snowmobile, because of the noise, the stink of the gasoline, and the difficulty of seeing and making little detours off the main trail in order to learn from the wilderness. During my first season as a trapper, I think I probably spent as much time sightseeing as I did on the business of gathering fur, never regretting one single moment of my truancy, for nature taught me a lot in this way.

There is a comment made by Alexander Graham Bell that so impressed me that I cut it out of the periodical in which it had been reproduced. I still have it; it reflects my own philosophies so perfectly and offers such good advice that I would like to include it here:

"Don't keep forever on the public road. Leave the beaten track occasionally and dive into the woods. You will be certain to find something worth thinking about to occupy your mind. All really big discoveries are the result of thought."

I have never made any really big discoveries, but I have made countless little ones as a result of diving into the woods, such as I did on a morning in spring, at ice-breakup time, when I left the main trail to get a better look at a ruffed grouse that was strutting under a tight clump of spruce trees. I watched the bird for a few minutes as it walked away, aware of my presence but believing itself sufficiently concealed and protected by the branchy trees to afford a leisurely retreat instead of bursting into quick, noisy flight.

When the bird had disappeared, I continued walking through the spruces instead of returning to the trail I had left, motivated by curiosity about the country and by the attraction

197 &

of the scene, particularly by the different shades of green that contrasted gently with patches of unmelted snow. This was muskeg country, an area where decayed vegetation covered the clay soils of antiquity to a depth of five feet or more before the chocolate-brown duff was itself carpeted by vividly green sphagnum moss that made walking comfortable and silent.

Such country is the bedroom of wolf and moose and deer, and the home of red squirrels and snowshoe hares and gray jays and chickadees that are stalked on the ground by the occasional lynx or bobcat and in the trees by the quick marten. Light is dim, for sunlight but rarely manages to filter through the canopy of spruce needles. Sound is muted, as though nature forbade all but whispers. Now and then the soft call of a chickadee is heard, or the plaintive, lonely whistle of a gray jay; occasionally a red squirrel challenges the stillness with its shrill call and all too rarely, but best of all sounds, the melancholy howl of a timber wolf floats through the land.

I walked slowly, pausing often to examine things of interest, noting a variety of tracks left in the melting snows and finding old bedding places of white-tailed deer, distinguishable from moose beds by their smaller circumference and by a scattering of shed hair. Once I found the meager remains of a snowshoe hare that had been pulled down and devoured by either a lynx or a bobcat. I could not determine which because the pug marks are so much alike, except for size, and the tracks I saw were too indistinct: lynx feet are generally larger than those of a bobcat, but a large "bob" will leave almost identical prints.

Although I had left home intending to gather all my traps from where I had left them sprung beside each set, a job that would take most of the day because of the scattered pattern of my trapline, I was in no hurry; indeed, time was of no consequence as I became involved with my surroundings. I can only say that I walked over the muskeg for about two hours before

I emerged into a more sparsely treed area where poplar and birch had secured a good hold and dominated the conifers.

About half a mile to the north I saw a small beaver pond, one that I did not know existed and which might offer a blanket or two next winter. I walked to it, moving quietly and keeping the cover of trees between myself and the water just in case some animal or bird was to be seen. When I was about fifty yards from the edge of the pond I heard loud hissing, now and then punctuated by the gnashing of teeth. Only a beaver could be making those noises; an angry beaver.

I walked forward with more care, pausing often to orient myself by the sounds, but before I caught sight of the noise-maker, a shrill scream of rage or pain stopped me in my tracks. I had not heard such a sound before, but I thought I knew its source, and because I was eager to confirm my suspicions, I moved with more speed than caution. My noisy passage over the last few yards of ground probably saved the life of a yearling beaver.

As I came in sight of the pond edge, I saw a large beaver savagely shaking a smaller animal into whose shoulder it had sunk its formidable incisors; the yearling beaver was bleeding profusely and wailing pitifully now, but the large animal held on and continued shaking viciously. The contest was being fought in water only about two inches deep and both animals were liberally covered with mud and blood.

My noisy arrival caused the large beaver to let go and to dash clumsily into deeper water, but the younger one was so bemused by shock and pain that it did not seem to realize that I was standing only about ten feet away. It stumbled onto dry land and walked slowly up the slight incline toward where I was standing, limping severely. I remained statue-still, not wanting to add to the poor animal's distress and hoping that it would pass me without becoming aware of my presence;

which was exactly what happened, giving me an opportunity to see more clearly the two slashes inflicted in its hide by the cutting teeth of the big beaver. I watched the yearling until it concealed itself in a clump of willows about fifty yards from where I stood, but I continued to listen to its slow movements for several more minutes.

When I could hear it no longer I walked down to the water's edge and looked at the scene of battle, reconstructing the happening as best I could. It seemed evident that the yearling had been ejected from its home pond, or perhaps it had left of its own accord, as they are wont to do, and had set out to find itself a new home.

The youngster may have checked several other likely places and found them already occupied before it reached the small pond; it may even have been involved in other, though less serious, clashes with adults before it was surprised by the big beaver.

Tracks in the soft ground on the edge of the pond told a fairly clear story. The yearling had come from the east, walking on land and slowly veering toward the water, until it had stopped at the very edge, front paws in the mud, back feet on the bank. Scanning this part of the pond, I saw a short, deep canal that sloped upward to emerge out of the water a few yards up the bank and very close to where the yearling had paused to inspect the pond. The big beaver had evidently entered the canal submerged, surfaced, and charged the young animal: the large tracks of the pond's defender were clearly printed on the edge of the canal, showing how the claws of one back foot had found purchase in the stiff mud and had actually dislodged a chunk of it as the beaver lunged at the intruder. Studying these marks, it looked as though the young animal had become suddenly aware of its danger and had spun around and tried to run, leaving telltale, elongated tracks; but before it had taken two steps the pond's owner had seized it. Evidently I had arrived shortly after the large beaver had made its charge, hissing loudly and gnashing its teeth; the rest of the action I had witnessed. I am fairly sure that if I had not arrived when I did, the pond's defender would have killed the intruder.

Such attacks on young beaver migrating in search of a new home are not uncommon, though they are not often witnessed, coming more usually to human notice with the discovery of a dead yearling floating on the water or, more rarely, washed ashore; on examination the cadavers show the wounds inflicted by the great teeth of their killers, fearful lacerations that testify to the fury of the attack as well as to the effectiveness of a beaver's weapons. On different occasions I have found three such dead yearlings, two in the water and one, partly eaten by other animals, some distance from the water. One of these had lost a front leg when the cutting teeth had bitten clean through the bone; another had been disemboweled when it had been attacked from underwater, its killer's teeth grasping its belly, sinking in, and tearing loose a piece of the stomach wall three inches wide by almost four inches long, a fierce and jagged wound through which the entrails had escaped.

Not all territorial disputes are as serious, but the majority of them result in bloodshed and few trapped beaver are found without old scars, especially on tail and ears, and although some of these old wounds may have been inflicted by unsuccessful predators, the majority probably stem from spring migration clashes.

A typical beaver colony in country not disturbed by humans, such as the one that I studied at Old Alec's Lake, is made up of the adult pair, last year's kits, and this year's litter, the number of young depending on the mother's age and condition and upon the survival rate among last year's litter, some of which are almost certainly picked off by predators or succumb to disease. In my opinion, the colony on Old Alec's Lake was fairly representative of other colonies elsewhere, except perhaps for the killing of the mother beaver by the wolf and the survival of Paddy, though such things are by no means rare.

It *is* rare for young beaver to remain in the home pond beyond their second year of life and common for them to leave the colony as soon as ice breakup occurs the spring after their birth, but this depends largely on conditions in and around the individual pond, stream, or lake. If the pond is large and the available food supply is good, the yearlings may well stay one more year with the family, even longer in rarer instances if the colony is small; but if there is overcrowding in relation to space and food supply, the yearlings will leave home, either of their own accord or forced out by the adults.

Such migrants may leave one at a time on different nights, or they may depart as a group and split up as they wander, so that only one or at most two of the young animals settle in one place. In any event, these migrations are always dangerous. Young, inexperienced, and slow-moving over land, the migrant beaver are exposed to the attacks of every meat eater in the wilderness in addition to the fury of their own kind if they blunder into an already occupied pond.

A study of beaver on Michipicoten Island in Lake Superior showed that out of 100 kits originally tagged, only 12 survived five years later, a mortality rate that may well be higher in other regions because there are no natural beaver predators on the island and the population had been untrapped previous to the study. This suggests that other beaver, defending their territory, and disease were the principal causes of mortality in that particular range.

Of course, in some areas, migrating yearlings may find many nearby water reservoirs that are unoccupied and that offer plentiful supplies of food. Under these conditions the survival rate would be higher because the migrants are more likely to avoid predators and other beaver, in addition to being less likely to succumb to disease when living on an adequate diet.

Despite the years that I have devoted to the study of beaver, I am not able to say how these animals find mates in the wild—and neither is anyone else, as far as I am aware. Most mammals show distinct external differences between male and female, but with beaver it is impossible to differentiate with the naked eye between a male and female and only an internal examination will readily determine an animal's sex. In addition, both males and females act in much the same way and are evidently equally aggressive in defense of their territory, so that with the exception of a nursing female, whose swollen mammary glands become obvious if she is seen *standing upright out of the water*, an observer cannot easily tell whether the animal he is watching is male or female.

Some people believe that beaver "pair up" in the home pond, but I find this unlikely because nature is usually careful about brother-sister matings, which may weaken the species. Raccoons illustrate this quite well (and so do many other species, of course): female raccoons are precocious and are usually ready to mate by the end of their first winter of life, while males remain immature until their second winter.

I lean toward the view that beaver males find mates much as do many other social animals, by going in search of them during the breeding season, braving the danger of predators and other beaver in this perennial quest, but aided in their search by the musk that is discharged by both sexes and which, to another beaver, probably differs in scent.

In other words, a lone female beaver traveling around the edge of her pond will discharge larger amounts of musk if she is receptive to a male, who quickly recognizes the special aroma and knows that he is close to a female.

However this may be, beaver are monogamous and evidently mate for life, though if one partner dies or is killed or trapped, the other is almost certain to seek another mate and it is perhaps for this reason that in some instances one or two subordinate adults are allowed to live in a colony; but such extra adults are *not allowed to mate*, the dominant female in the pond preventing any other females from soliciting a male and the dominant male controlling the fervor of any single males in the colony.

At this stage of man's knowledge of beaver affairs in untrapped regions, it would seem that beaver live a relatively long life, perhaps more than twenty years once they have become established in a good pond, though accidents, disease, and predation may reduce the average lifespan to as little as four or five years at times.

Mating usually takes place in the water, though it may also take place on top of the ice, but little is known about the animal's courting rituals. I have seen beaver standing in shallow water with their arms around each other, but this has been late in the season, after breakup, so it is unlikely that the animals were observing any more than an exchange of affection, for mating usually occurs in January or February, when the ponds in the northern part of their range are frozen over.

The gestation period is between 100 and 110 days, and the kits are usually born in April or May, depending on the latitude of their range, which also probably governs the actual time of mating—earlier in the south than in the north. At birth kits may weigh as little as eight or as much as twenty-five ounces, with the average probably reaching one pound. Kits come into the world on a makeshift bed of damp grasses, rootlets, and other vegetation with their eyes open and a good covering of soft fur on their bodies. (Incidentally, the kit's "bed" is usually eaten by the youngsters within a few days of birth.)

An intriguing characteristic of this extraordinary animal is that it practices birth control, in that it is able to regulate population numbers to conform with the available food supply and the mortality rate in a particular colony, a trait that evidently also has bearing on the migration of the young beaver, which are more likely to be allowed to linger in a colony that has become depleted because of trapping, natural predation, or disease.

Just how this natural birth-control program works is not known, but it is a fact that in untrapped colonies which have stable populations, few females will accept the attentions of the males and those that *do* breed have smaller litters. But if colony numbers drop, all females mate and have larger litters. Interestingly, this characteristic of the beaver is shared by the wolf, which regulates its pack numbers in the same way.

If wolves are left undisturbed by man, and if living conditions are good, the dominant, or alpha, female in each pack prevents the submissive females from mating and she herself gives birth to fewer pups. If, on the other hand, the wolves are trapped or poisoned, or if game has been scarce in any one year and starvation has reduced the pack numbers, all females mate and the litters are larger. There may be some significance in the fact that beaver form an important part of a wolf's diet during the frost-free months, so that the predators may have contributed to the beaver's practice of increasing its litters in the face of adversity and the beaver, in times of population scarcity, may have influenced the wolf's practice of increasing the size of the pack by having more young.

In any event, the rule for both these animals appears to be: when the living is easy, exercise birth control for the good of the colony or the pack, but when the living is tough, *increase* the population; and if at first glance this may appear to work in reverse, logical reflection will show that beaver and wolf have hit upon the right way to balance their populations.

Both species are social animals that live in clearly defined home territories, and although the diet of each is diametrically opposite, both nevertheless are entirely dependent upon the food supplies furnished by their range, just as the inhabitants of a nation depend upon their farmland to grow food. If the economy is stable and there is no other threat to the well-being of pack or colony, it is in the interest of each species to balance its population so that it keeps pace with the food supply; but if the economy becomes unstable and results in a reduction of population through starvation, disease, or predation, the species is threatened with extinction and must increase its numbers in order to ensure the survival of enough individuals in years ahead.

Because life in the wild has always been faced by periods of feast followed by periods of famine, nature evidently decreed eons ago that she would be careful of the species and careless of the individual. To achieve this, *all* species were made sensitive to population fluctuations. This sensitivity affects the urge to breed and, in social animals, produces an inborn urge to regulate the numbers of the unit, even in normal times; it is for this latter reason that beaver young are made to migrate in search of their own home ponds, just as surplus young in a wolf pack leave the family and join other, depleted packs or find a mate who is similarly alone, when the two form their own pack on a suitable range.

These population checks and balances are found among all wild animals, even though they do not always work in the same way. This accounts for the suicidal and seemingly senseless mass migration of the lemmings when they reach a population peak and for the equally suicidal decline among snowshoe hares when these animals reach the point of population explosion, to quote but two other examples. Does it also account for the Biblical parable that warns of the seven fat years followed by seven years of famine? Sometimes it seems to me that nature is trying to teach my own species a lesson in simple mathematics: how to multiply, divide, and *subtract*.

With most animals, and especially in the case of beaver, the subtraction of numbers among populations undisturbed by man hinges on any one of the three principal causes that I have mentioned: food supply, predation, or disease, not necessarily in that order. Individuals may succumb as a result of any one of these, or as a result of a combination of two or all three. When death results from predation or starvation, it is readily apparent, but this is not so with disease, which may be the sole factor in a death or may be a secondary factor.

Beaver are prone to a number of bacterial diseases, the most serious being tularemia, a condition caused by the bacterium *Pasteurella tularensis* and spread through infection between beaver or by the bite of a blood-sucking insect that has previously come into contact with a tularemia-infected animal. It affects the liver and spleen, and infected animals show characteristic white spots on these organs. The disease, incidentally, also affects man, who can contract it by handling infected animals. Sometimes outbreaks of tularemia virtually wipe out a beaver population, as was the case in Ontario in the 1950's, when the animals nearly became extinct in the northwestern part of the province.

Significantly, such parasitic diseases become more common and play the greatest havoc when populations are at their peak, and for this reason ecologists refer to them as being *density-dependent*—parasites can travel from host to host with greater ease. After the epidemic is over, populations spring right back, and beaver multiply rapidly until they reach the point of balance once more.

Other parasites that affect beaver in less measure, and in some cases not at all, are flatworms and roundworms that live in the stomach, intestines, and even the body cavity of beaver. The animals are also unwitting hosts to external parasites such as ticks and leeches. One curious little creature that makes its home on the beaver is a minute beetle that I have not been able to identify (mostly because I have been too busy with other things to devote time to it) and which is often found in large numbers crawling about in the animal's fur. From my own experience, and talking to other trappers about it, it appears that this little mite causes no damage to the fur or to the beaver, and this seems to be the accepted view of biologists, according to a paper that I read recently on the subject. Since nobody else has come up with a theory accounting for the habits of this beetle, I'd like to propose my own, arrived at, strangely enough, through my observations of hawks.

The young of predatory birds, helpless in their nests until they are able to fly and raised on a diet of raw meat, would quickly become fouled by decay and their own excreta if it were not for a couple of simple and sensible provisions of nature, always a careful housekeeper. Young hawks, or eyases, as they are called, grow rapidly, eat ravenously, and defecate copiously; to avoid soiling the nest, these birds come equipped with special rectal muscles that allow them to expel a stream of feces with great force. To defecate, the eyases stand up, cock their tails upward, and let fly, the stream of excreta sailing neatly over the edge of the nest.

I have observed this many times and on several occasions I was not quick enough to get out of the way. I can testify that the stream can strike with surprising impact and spread even when the "target" is standing ten feet away. But while I was familiar with this housekeeping habit of raptors, I was totally unaware of a second "sanitary system" common to the birds (I have not yet seen it mentioned by other observers) until I found an injured eyas that had tried to fly before it was ready. It was a red-tailed hawk, almost fully fledged and quite large, and it had dislocated its elbow joint.

I popped the bone in place and kept the bird until its wing

was strong enough for flight three weeks later. It was just after I had treated the eyas that I noticed a maggot crawling around among its head feathers. My instinctive reaction was to pick it off and get rid of it, feeling as I did the usual repugnance for these "rot worms," but my curiosity overcame my repugnance and I watched the maggot, wondering how it had managed to get into the hawk's feathers, and why.

Presently I saw another worm, in the neck feathers, and yet another appeared on the right wing, the one I had doctored. Now I became interested in earnest and I ran to get a magnifying glass. The maggot on the wing was closest to me and I concentrated on it first; to my amazement I noticed that the little pallid worm was carefully eating decayed matter that adhered to the hawk's feathers. I put the other maggots under the glass while the hawk kept one fierce eye glued on me: all the maggots were busy eating decayed matter, cleaning the stuff from the bird's feathers.

The simplicity and efficacy of the operation were obvious; once more I was impressed by nature's superlative house-keeping—if there wasn't some way of ridding the birds of carrion, their feathers would become so matted that they would probably never learn how to fly.

That was ten years ago, and since then I have seen a lot more nestling raptors, all of which had their complement of crawling maggots, which were often eaten by the hawks after they fell out of the feathers, replete with the carrion they had removed.

The maggots on the hawks led me to theorize that the beetles on the beaver serve a similar purpose by living off the decayed vegetation that works its way deep down under the fur, material that would be difficult for the beaver to remove, despite the animal's careful grooming. I am not yet able to document this view, because the best opportunity that I have ever had to study these beetles was when I found Paddy and in those days I assumed that the parasites were harmful and I spent time ridding the kit of his tenants. Before and since that time I only encountered the beetles on newly killed beaver, but perhaps one day I will get another opportunity to study the mites properly.

Fifteen The afternoon was sunny and cool, one of those clear mid-September days that are the prelude to the kaleidoscope of a northland autumn. I sat on Spring Rock watching Paddy, now an accepted member of the beaver colony, who was swimming across the lake with one of the older kits. Both were heading toward Perch Bay, evidently intending to feed on the abundant water-lily roots that grew in its shallows.

The lake sparkled clean in the sunshine, a crystal cup of liquid that was undisturbed but for the slowly tumbling wake made by the swimming beaver, an enormous mirror that reflected the images of blue sky and green growth and the rugged gray of ancient granite. Paddy and his brother stroked in a leisurely manner, their squarish heads with their pricked ears the only parts of their bodies revealed to my eyes. I looked for several minutes, noting details of their surface movements, while my peripheral vision registered the beauty of the scene, the peace of it; my mind fogged with fantasy, with the dreams of day that replace reality. It was almost as though my physical self wasn't there at all, as though I was sitting in a darkened theater watching an enchanting scene projected in Technicolor on a wide screen. And then the vision passed.

Soon, said an intruding ghost voice, I would have to leave this place, perhaps never to come back, never to see Paddy again. I wasn't exactly sad as I recovered my full faculties, but I entered a mood of premature nostalgia produced by the sudden realization that I had little time left in which to contemplate the wondrous sights of beaver country. And yet, now that I had returned to the moment, I could not help looking forward to being with my own kind again, to talk to *people*, sitting in my small apartment and sipping an ice-cold drink while catching up with the news and discussing affairs of the world with friends newly dropped in to welcome me back.

It was like waking up after a very pleasant dream and realizing that the new day was to bring an exciting change to one's life, when, in that drugged semi-awake state, one tries desperately to cling to the dream while also trying to focus on actuality. It took a conscious effort of will to return my mind to the task at hand.

I had climbed the rock vantage in order to sit quietly and to complete my notes on the events that had taken place during the last few weeks, a task that I had neglected lately.

The last entry in my notebook recorded my shopping trip to Mother's store and some of the highlights of her story of Alfred and his trapping accident, at the close of which I had jotted down a few of the observations that I had made on the trip back to Old Alec's Lake. Since then, I had been too carefree to listen to the voice of discipline and I had lived indulgently from day to day. Now I had myself in hand once more and I concentrated on my task.

During the time that had passed since my shopping trip, Paddy had gained full confidence in himself and had become totally at home in his proper world, a change of nature that may have developed gradually but which manifested itself almost instantly when I took down his fence and allowed him to wander at will. As I had promised to do before going out to Mother's, I dismantled his nursery the evening of my return, my every action closely supervised by the kit. He showed great curiosity in my doings and made a point of inspecting each posthole the moment that I yanked the pole out of the ground.

When I was finished and had stacked the posts near the tent for use as fuel, and when the chicken wire had been rolled up and placed on the beach in readiness for its return to the outside, I put fresh wood on the fire and sat beside it, drinking tea and waiting to see what Paddy would do now that he could please himself.

For a time he sat on his tail beside me, scratching a bit, twitching his ears, scenting the air, as was his habit, while his eyes seemed to be drawn into the heart of the flames. Once, the buck swam near our shoreline, but he didn't come close, and although Paddy turned to look at his father, he showed no other signs of interest. Half an hour later, just as I was beginning to believe that Paddy didn't know what to do with his freedom, the two older kits surfaced some fifty yards from shore.

Paddy got off his tail, stood on all fours facing the water, sniffed once, and waddled to the shoreline. With hardly a pause he entered the lake silently and started to swim toward the adolescent beavers. I watched anxiously. The three animals met, sniffed each other, and dived in unison, Paddy's smaller bulk sandwiched between the other two. It was as simple as that; it was as though this moment had been ordained, a natural reunion that just had to be.

I don't know how long they remained underwater, perhaps a couple of minutes, but when they surfaced they had traveled about a hundred yards in the direction of Water Lily Bay, toward which they continued to swim. Five minutes later they entered East Creek and disappeared from view.

"That's that," I muttered. It was a sort of farewell to Paddy; now I was sure that he had been accepted by the colony but I wasn't sure that he would return to me again. I would miss him, but I was happy for him, even if I felt a little depressed over his leaving.

To take my mind off his departure, I went for a walk in the gathering dusk, crossing Deer Valley and Blueberry Flats in an aimless ramble that lasted about an hour and a half. It was full dark when I got back to the silent camp; the lake was calm but for the small ripples caused by a slight breeze. I supposed that Paddy was somewhere in one of the marshes, feeding with his family.

That night the moon was full. When it had risen high enough to illuminate the lake, I climbed Spring Rock with the glasses, aware within myself that I hoped to catch sight of Paddy, but ostensibly intent on studying the lake during moonlight. After a full scan of the lake, the movement that rewarded my scrutiny was made by a small flotilla of ducks swimming toward shelter in the cattails south of the dams and by one loon that bobbed up and down silently as it rode the slight current near Bass Island and by the tiny, spreading circles produced when small fish nosed up to the surface to pick up some edible bit of flotsam. The wilderness was almost completely silent, not even the buzzing of mosquitoes was audible;

the deciduous leaves rustled very gently and there was the shishing of small waves against the rocky shore; that was all.

I went to bed wondering if Paddy would come home tomorrow to get his feed of formula and I worried a little about him, but I was also relieved that he had returned to his own. I was as fond of him as ever and I didn't care for the thought of finally parting from him, but I had to confess that taking care of the kit for so long had been a major responsibility that had hindered my freedom to a greater extent than I had realized until now.

Lying in my sleeping bag watching the shadows of leaves etched on the tent roof by the moonlight, I pushed away my emotions and thought about my sudden and unexpected guardianship of Paddy with the naturalist's objectivity. Certainly, caring for him had been a task that I would not have chosen to undertake on a field trip like this had I thought about it before my discovery of the female beaver's remains. I would have felt that being a foster parent under these conditions would severely hamper my movement; which, of course, it did. Yet I had learned a great deal from the young beaver and through him I had also been afforded an ideal opportunity to study the other members of the colony at close range, accepting me as they did because of the kit's influence. On balance, then, what began as an altruistic, emotional decision to save the kit had yielded knowledge that I could not have acquired under any other circumstances in such a comparatively short space of time. Additionally, the human being that—in my case, at any rate—always lurks beneath the exterior of the naturalist, had found reward and pleasure in the friendship and affection given so freely by the kit.

I felt satisfaction over my success in raising Paddy and I was happy for him now that he had rejoined his family; but the reality of the situation was clear: my job was done and I was free of the responsibility it entailed. I drifted off into a relaxed sleep, content with the knowledge that I would see Paddy again.

At breakfast next morning I sat munching raisin bannocks laced with marmalade, sipping good coffee between mouthfuls, and basking in the combined warmth of sun and fire. The birds were in good voice, especially a wood thrush in a thicket of spruce about two hundred yards away, near Deer Valley, who was launching his beautiful melody as though he intended it for my personal pleasure. The lake was quiet; very quiet. I was struck by its emptiness, for hitherto the buck would come around at about this time, making his last call on me (as I had liked to think) before he sought rest in his lodge. Today, for the first time since I rescued Paddy, not a single beaver was in sight, and I had to admit that the buck's interest in the camp had centered on his son. At any rate, the pattern had now been broken; it was to remain so for the rest of my stay at Old Alec's Lake.

The other beaver did not become suddenly shy, and when I met them when I was out in the canoe, they did not dive or panic; they merely kept clear of me and continued on their own course. The buck would still drop by once in a while, but he stayed a hundred yards or so from shore, looking my way curiously and swimming slowly before altering course for some other part of the lake. The older kits, who had visited Paddy almost daily of late, did not come at all, and neither did the shy young female.

But Paddy did. He arrived in camp the evening after his release, ambled toward me, stopped to shake his coat to rid it of excess moisture, then came to me to stand on his hind legs, looking up. I stroked his head, went to pick him up, but he avoided my reaching hands; it seemed that he was content to be stroked and scratched, enjoying this as much as ever, but he did not want to be picked up any more. I chuckled; he reminded me of an adolescent boy who suddenly decides that being hugged by his father is kid stuff.

During the next two weeks Paddy called on me every evening for a feed of Pablum and a bit of scratch and tickle; then his visits became irregular, sometimes occurring every other evening, at other times missing for three or four, then showing up and staying an hour or so before returning to the lake. By the middle of September his visits became sporadic; he might show up at breakfast, instead of suppertime, lick up half a cup of formula, and leave, not to return for several days. I often watched him swim across the lake with one or more of the other beaver, as I was doing that afternoon from Spring Rock, and occasionally I would meet him on the lake, when he always responded to my call and steered himself so that he swam alongside the canoe, looking up at me, communicating in his own way, and staying for a little time.

By now the weather had turned chilly, even cold, at night and during early morning as a rime of ice on the edges of spring and lake attested; and some of the deciduous trees were changing the color of their leaves, the poplars turning pale yellow, the crowns of the red maples daubed scarlet. The evening before, I heard the clamor of geese, the sound of their shrill voices approaching from the north. I was sitting beside the comfort of my fire and I looked up in time to see the Canadas sail over the trees, losing height rapidly, aiming for Water Lily Bay; soon the leading gander let down his undercarriage and began to break speed by flapping his great wings downward. The rest of the wedge followed closely, copying their leader's actions. About fifty geese splashed into the bay, gossiping noisily, going through the jerky movements of settling in the water with much tail wagging and head bobbing.

According to the arbitrary calculations of science, autumn was not due to arrive until the twenty-third day of this month, but the weather and the trees and the geese were clearly unaware of this. As far as I was concerned, autumn was here already and I would soon have to break camp and head out.

That afternoon, after I had watched Paddy and his brother swim to Perch Bay, I climbed down, went to the tent, picked up a fresh notebook, and turned toward Blueberry Flats, from where I kept walking until I reached the area of the northern ponds. I wanted to see if the beaver in those colonies had begun to cut their winter supply of poplar; it was a little early for this kind of activity, perhaps, but I was in the mood for a quiet walk and I also wanted to time the cutting activities of the three colonies, to see if they all began more or less simultaneously, a discovery that I never made.

Because of the emphasis that is placed on the cutting of trees by beaver, many people believe that these animals live entirely on a diet of wood; I had been no exception in this when I was in Europe, influenced in the belief by the writings on the subject; it was not until I met Old Alec that I learned differently. In fact, beaver enjoy a wide variety of plants during spring, summer, and early autumn, turning to the bark of trees only when ground vegetation begins to die.

The actual amount of wood consumed by beaver is minimal and usually accidental, ingested unavoidably when an animal cuts down a tree or when it is gnawing off the bark that forms the bulk of its diet in winter, though the animals also feed on underwater plants at this time, particularly the roots of water lilies, succulent tubers to which I am myself partial in the fall. They make a good substitute for potato and when eaten boiled or roasted are a nice change of camp diet. The Indians, incidentally, used to grind them into flour with which they made a kind of unleavened bread.

Beaver are known to use practically every species of tree and bush that grows on their range, the kind selected depending on the availability of the species and on the likes and dislikes of individual animals. Where it is available, poplar, or aspen as it is also called, appears to be a favorite, probably because the genus *Populus* is widespread on this continent and furnishes a variety of species, such as trembling aspen, large-toothed aspen, balsam poplar, black cottonwood, lance-leaf cottonwood, eastern cottonwood, plains cottonwood, and narrow-leaf cottonwood. Usually, these broad-leafed trees spring up wherever logging has reduced evergreen stands, and it is possible that lumbering operations during the early days of settlement by white immigrants, who were anxious to clear land for farming and to cut down evergreens for construction of their log homes, have encouraged the spread of *Populus* and influenced the diet of beaver as a result.

However this may be, beaver are found living in areas of North America where the poplar does not exist and, conversely, they are found in areas where they have a choice of poplar and other types of trees, in which locations they do not appear to discriminate solely in favor of poplar. If a colony lives in an area where only one or two species of tree grow, it has little choice, but where stands are mixed, it will eat maple, birch, oak, beech, cherry, alder, spruce, pine, cedar, hemlock, or fir, according to individual taste and distance of the trees from the water. Because they feel insecure cutting a long way from the pond, beaver will first use those trees that grow close to the water, especially in areas where the ground is unsuited for the building of canals.

At one time it was believed that beaver could influence the direction in which a tree would fall, and the animals were thought to plan so that the trees dropped toward the water, where they could cut them up safely and more conveniently. This is not so. (The reason for this belief evidently came from the fact that it is not unusual for trees growing near the water to lean toward it because branch growth tends to be heavier on the side facing the water and cut trees are pulled over by this weight, though this is by no means always the case.) In fact, trees drop any which way at all; many of them never make it all the way to the ground, but get hung up on other trees instead. I have seen some patches of country where the hung-up trees formed an almost impassable barrier and where the beaver must have had to work twice as hard to get food.

This used to puzzle me at first. Nature is not usually wasteful and this untidy state of affairs seemed to suggest a kind of wanton destruction found only in the wake of man's passage, but after years of tracking through the wilderness during which I found many areas where hung-up trees existed in varying stages of decomposition, I realized that there was, after all, a purpose in the disorder; in time the dead trees are returned to the soil and produce mulch which enriches the earth and allows other species of plant to flourish. Additionally and significantly, trees get hung up only in those places where the timber stand *needs thinning out*, where the growth is so thick that none of the trees is able to attain proper growth. Under such conditions, trees grow tall and thin, being too close together to allow for proper development; they are exposed to the danger of high winds that are likely to flatten entire stands because the girth of the trunk and spread of root do not compensate for height and the trees are loosely anchored in the soil.

In northern parts of their range, where extreme cold isolates the beaver from its food supply, the animals must stock a sufficient number of cut logs underwater to last through the winter, sinking them before the ice begins to form. The winter larder is usually located near the lodge at a sufficient depth to keep it from freezing and the logs are either rammed hard into the mud (if they are thin and light enough for the beaver to handle in this way) or weighted down with stones.

This intriguing habit, eminently sensible though it is, poses an interesting question: Is the beaver able to determine in advance the amount of supplies needed to keep it through the winter? The answer is no; the animal cannot forecast the length of winter and it cannot compute the girth of the logs it has cut or measure their length, which it would have to do in order to determine how much bark the pile would yield. But though it cannot estimate its needs and does not know how much food to cut and store, the beaver never starves to death. In fact, there is usually food left over in the larder when spring arrives.

What happens is that beaver "slow down" in winter; they are influenced by the long hours of darkness—at best, even out of their lodges, they inhabit a world of semi-light, covered as they are by a thick layer of ice topped by snow. Body functions slow down under these conditions and the animals go for varying periods (sometimes for days at a time) without eating. This is not true hibernation, however, and the beaver's body temperature drops only a few degrees from normal, but it is a sort of semi-hibernation common to a number of other northland animals, who go through similar periods of inactivity during which they survive without food as their bodies consume the extra fat that has been put on during late summer and fall. Bears are well known for this, and so are raccoons.

Beaver move about more during winter than these other animals, but they are by no means as active as they are in spring, summer, and autumn; and they require less food, being furnished instead with extra layers of body fat, which is a useful source of fuel when the animals become torpid.

During days of clear skies and strong sunshine that is diffused through the roof of ice and snow, the beaver become active and feed on their underwater supplies; on cloudy days they are more likely to remain in their lodges, almost totally inactive. And of course, because of the longer nights of winter, they spend many more hours at rest in their nesting chambers.

At times during autumn, for reasons that still elude me, beaver may cut down trees and then leave them on land, storing only a few in their underwater larder. On other occasions a colony may drop three or four large trees (depending on the number of animals involved) in addition to a quantity of willows and alders or saplings that are cut into manageable lengths and carried underwater. On yet other occasions, the colony may cut down fifteen or twenty medium to small trees. On the average, the animals use trees that vary between four and fourteen inches across the butt, working remarkably quickly, able to chew down a tree five or six inches thick at the stump in three to four minutes.

Now and then a beaver tackles a tree, gnaws it halfway through, and leaves it, never returning to finish the job. On these occasions work may be abandoned because the logger has been disturbed and later forgets where it was cutting and begins anew somewhere else. Usually beaver work alone, but they may combine to cut down a very large tree, so that if one animal starts to cut down an average-size tree and doesn't finish the job, the chances are that another beaver from the colony will not pick up where the other one left off if it comes across one of these freshly gnawed, but still-standing trees, because it believes that the original cutter will return to its task. By the time a few days have gone by and the cut has dried out, even the beaver that began the job will avoid the old chop.

There does not seem to be any limit to the size of trees that beaver will tackle. In one place, I found a stump that measured 61 inches across the butt, and the crown, part of which was left lying where it had fallen, was 106 feet away from the stump; allowing for a couple of feet of distance between stump and butt, a gap created by the bounce of the fallen giant, the tree measured, when standing, 104 feet. Other observers have reported even larger trees cut down by beaver.

If the tree is a big one and does not suddenly snap and fall, the beaver is apt to run away from it as it begins to sway downward, making for the water if this is nearby, or running in the opposite direction to the trunk's movement and then heading back to canal or pond after the tree has landed. This action is not induced by fear of the tree falling on the cutter, but by fear of predators being attracted to the site by the resounding crash made when the tree hits the ground, for the hunters have learned to associate this noise with the presence of beaver on land. As a result, the beaver seeks refuge in the water after a large tree has fallen and it patrols up and down, sniffing and listening, not to re-emerge on land until it feels it is safe to do so. I am inclined to think that not all beaver behave in this fashion, especially those living in proximity to man in areas where major predators, such as wolves or cougar, have been eliminated. Under such conditions, the beaver knows perfectly well that it is not liable to attack, or that it can cope with the minor threat posed by the smaller meat eaters, such as bobcat or fox, which will think twice before facing the formidable incisors of a beaver turned at bay.

During autumn cutting, beaver often feed off the bark on land and it is not unusual to find trees that have been gnawed bare but which have not been cut up into lengths. As often, beaver cut off the branches of a large tree and carry them to their larder, leaving the heavy trunk on shore and returning to it later to feed off the bark. In the spring, at ice-breakup time, and before significant fresh plant growth appears, beaver turn to young trees for their food. Saplings an inch or two at the stump will be cut down, carried to shallow water, and stripped of their tender, sap-heavy bark, which is consumed with relish. Some tree cutting is also done in summer by individual animals, who seem to prefer to vary their plant diet with a little succulent bark, but this is more unusual, most animals preferring to eat plant growth until late autumn.

Tree-cutting activities usually cease shortly before freeze-up, after which the beaver remain under the ice or in their lodges, secure from their enemies when swimming and kept warm when at rest inside the chambers, for even when the temperature registers below zero outside, the lodges are so well insulated with mud, sticks, and plant growth that the temperature inside them is maintained several degrees above freezing by the body heat of the animals. Protected as they are by their dense fur coats, beaver experience no discomfort from the cold.

When a good sheet of ice forms over the pond, the beaver resort to a trick that almost cost me my life in the winter of 1956, when I was logging for a living, selling pulpwood to the Minnesota-Ontario Pulp and Paper Company in Fort Frances. I had finished cutting in one part of my property and had to move operations across a wide creek that bisected my land from north to south and which I had already crossed many times on my tractor.

On the day in question, I had risen at dawn in order to collect my equipment, load it on a trailer, and take the lot with the tractor across the creek to set up a base of operations on the other side, in an area that I had previously scouted. By then I was wise enough to the quirks of a northland winter to avoid taking chances, and during earlier trips over the ice that covered the southward-running waterway, I had first tested the thickness of the gel, cutting a hole and measuring. I knew there were at least nine inches of ice between my tractor and the water; I had made sure of this two weeks earlier and the temperature had dropped considerably since then. Ice this thick could easily take the weight of the tractor, both in theory and in fact. When I arrived that fateful morning, I had no hesitation in steering the machine onto the ice and following the waterway's course southward.

I was in the center of the creek when an ominous groan told me that the ice was giving way. Before I had time to do more than open the throttle in the hope of gaining hard ground as rapidly as possible, a series of loud cracks signaled the collapse of my ice bridge. Down went the tractor.

I stayed glued to the seat, my horrified eyes fixed on the brown, swirling water that rose rapidly, caused the exhaust pipe to make dull bubbling sounds, and then all too soon killed the engine. To say that I was scared is to understate my true feelings as I watched the tractor continue to sink and the ice-cold water begin to rise over my feet, up my legs, my thighs, my seat. Mercifully, the big back wheels touched the muddy bottom at last and the machine settled in the water at a drunken angle.

I was alone, six miles away from my nearest neighbor, and when I had left the house earlier the thermometer registered 28 degrees below zero. Obviously I couldn't stay on the tractor, but the distance to either shore was too far to jump and I was afraid that any sudden movement would cause the machine to sink more deeply. For seconds that seemed to drag on like hours, I remained still, my legs lifted as high as possible to avoid further contact with the water.

In the end I had no choice in the matter. I had to get off the machine, trust to the treachery of floating lumps of ice, and attempt to fling myself ashore. I almost made it, too, taking short, quick strides from ice floe to ice floe, but some three feet from the bank, in I went, up to the chest in water that could not have been more than a couple of degrees above freezing. Luckily I was close enough to shore to be able to scramble out.

I started to run as fast as I possibly could, realizing that only in exercise lay survival until I could get inside the house, strip off my clothes, and huddle beside the stove. I had three miles to go.

I was lucky. I made it back without any lasting ill effects, though my clothes froze solid and parts of my pants cracked and lacerated my legs. But I was blue with cold and I had the shakes, so violently, in fact, that I was barely able to put fresh logs into the fire and coax life into it. It took an hour to get warm again, an hour of agony, beginning first in my toes and fingers and rising slowly up my legs until it reached my waist: a deep dull ache, worse than toothache; then a pain as though I had burned myself and lastly an attack of pins and needles such as I had never experienced before and never wish to again.

The two stiff gulps of neat whiskey that I took helped in one way and hindered in another. They warmed me inside, all right, but coming on top of an empty stomach, they got me quite drunk, which may have been just as well, but nevertheless did not improve my efficiency when I went to the barn to harness Dick, my enormous part Belgian, part scrub logging horse—an animal that knew more about the business than I did.

I had to get Dick back to the creek and salvage the tractor at once, before it froze in solid, or it would remain there until spring and become hopelessly ruined. Dick, long-suffering fellow, put up with my fumbling and with the silly giggles that I couldn't stop making as a result of raw whiskey and near hysteria; I believe the horse even did his best to help! When I had finished, I left Dick in the barn while I returned to the house and made some strong coffee, gulping two mugs of the stuff and putting the remainder in a thermos flask to take along with me. As I went to get Dick, I looked at the thermometer: the temperature had fallen to 38 below zero.

I will dwell lightly with our struggle to free the tractor. Dick worked like a Trojan; so did I. Before I could hitch chains to the tractor, I had to cut two trees long enough to span the creek, and when Dick had dragged them to the edge of the ice, I freed the chains from the horse's harness, left them attached to the logs, and tied a long length of baling twine to their free ends; tying a stick to the baling twine, I threw it across the creek; then I mounted the horse and we detoured a mile in order to get to the other side over dry land.

I pulled the twine, got the chains across, hitched them to Dick, and he heaved the logs over, making a crude but effective bridge. Now I could go and fasten the chains to the tractor. Three hours later the machine was on land.

The bush gods were with me that day. Feeling that I was wasting my time, I turned the engine over with the hand crank; once, twice, three times. The engine caught, coughed, spluttered, and settled down to a ragged beat. I gave it a quarter throttle and waited five minutes; the engine settled down to its normal pitch. Now I unharnessed Dick and told him to go home; once he was on his way I climbed into the tractor and followed.

In the yard, I dismounted, leaving the engine running while I put Dick back in the barn, rubbed him down well, and gave him a feed of oats as a reward for his wonderful efforts. Outside I got into the driver's seat again and began to run the tractor around the yard, hoping to clear the ice that had accumulated in the axles and wheel bearings. Around and around that yard I went for two hours before the crunch, crunch of ice ceased and the machine appeared to be acting normally. I was freezing cold when I put the tractor in its shed and fled to the house. Now the temperature had dropped to 53 *degrees below zero*, the coldest known in that country for many years.

For two days the big cold lasted. I stayed close to the fire and did nothing but thank the gods for my escape while I tried to understand the cause of my nearly fatal accident. When the weather moderated at last, I got my snowshoes and tramped over to the creek, ax in hand, determined to test the ice again at various points. When I arrived at the scene of the accident, the only remaining signs of the happening were two or three humps in the otherwise smooth surface of the ice. I started cutting a hole, measuring inch by inch as I went down; at eleven inches I broke through, but not into water. There was an eighteen-inch air space between ice and creek water. I had driven my tractor on ice suspended only by the creek banks!

That was how I learned that beaver, wise creatures, wait until they have a good strong roof of ice over their pond, then let out a foot or two of water to create an air space that allows them to breathe while they swim under the ice. Were it not for this air space (which I have found in numerous ponds in different parts of Canada) beaver would have to depend for their oxygen on air pockets trapped under the ice, and although in some places they must take advantage of these pockets, it is at best a risky business. By deliberately breaching their dam at the right time and letting some of the water escape downstream, beaver assure themselves of air space while they swim in their ice-bound home.

After my return from the northern ponds the afternoon that I went to see if the beaver there were beginning to cut down trees—which they were not yet doing—I was carrying a snowshoe-hare buck that I had shot on Blueberry Flats, an unexpected bonus brought down by a lucky shot from the .22 rifle I had taken with me as an afterthought when I went to pick up my notebook. I had not eaten fresh meat for a number of weeks and that supper was a gala affair.

I skinned and cleaned the hare and stuffed it with a mixture of chopped dried apples and raisins bound together by oatmeal and kept inside the body cavity by a couple of twists of fine wire. Then I spitted the carcass on a green willow and roasted it on the open fire, rotating it slowly and drooling at the aroma. When all was ready I set to; I am not ashamed to say that I ate the entire hare in one meal and afterward savored a compote of dried apples and prunes, the whole washed down with aromatic black coffee. I retired to bed totally gorged that night, the first time I had gone to sleep on a really full belly since I came to Old Alec's Lake.

The next day I began to study my notes and to correlate the new material they contained, elaborating wherever necessary and putting together an abbreviated account of my stay and adventures in this corner of beaver country. It was a time-consuming job that kept me busy almost continuously, my only relief coming at mealtime and at night and on those occasions when Paddy arrived to keep me company for a while and to sample a little Pablum and milk.

The kit had grown considerably in the last month and weighed, I estimated, a good thirty pounds, a rate of growth that put him well ahead of other beaver his age, if one could trust the estimates of those observers who have kept weight records (which I have never kept); according to these, beaver kits attain a weight of between eleven and twenty-eight pounds by the time that ice comes to sheet the ponds. Paddy looked as though he could already top the maximum weight and there was a while to go yet before Old Alec's Lake would be completely icebound.

One morning I got up to find that the first snow had fallen. About two inches of sheer white covered the country right down to water's edge; judging by the sullen sky, more was to come before the day was out.

I tried to compute the date, but the best I could do was to guess that this was about the end of the first week of October, give or take a few days. But I didn't need to guess to know that it was time to leave Old Alec's Lake. Any night now the frost could come in earnest and I might wake up one morning to find that the country was frozen over.

If this should happen, I would find myself in helpless isolation for several weeks, depending on the temperature and the rate of freeze-up, for there is a period that can last from three to six weeks when canoe travel is impossible because the ice is too heavy to allow passage and yet is too fragile to take the weight of a man. In any event, I had not brought my snowshoes—I mean, who thinks about snowshoes in May!

That morning I began to pack up, gathering first the things that were outside the tent, then sorting my gear inside. By the time I had finished, had got all my effects piled in their proper packing order, more snow was falling, driven in small, sharp flakes by a brisk northwest wind that made wasps out of the tiny flakes. I didn't want to leave here under these conditions. I wanted to wait until the weather cleared so that I could paddle away in the brightness of sunshine sparkling on fresh-fallen snow.

I unfolded my sleeping bag and set it back down in its accustomed corner and I got enough food out of my packs to do me for another couple of days; the rest of my gear I left at the ready and I spent the remainder of that day huddled close to the fire, shoulders draped by my canvas parka, the only really warm garment that I had brought with me, staring often at the sky and willing the clouds to disperse. Of course, there were no beaver about during the storm.

The snow stopped falling during the night. It was replaced by a sudden and sharp frost that left a quarter of an inch of ice on the edges of the lake. But the sun rose bright in the morning and the sky was of a blue unrivaled and the wild geese flew high overhead, a great formation of them, crying their special farewell to the northland.

Now was the time to leave. I did. In half an hour I had packed the canoe, struck the tent and stuffed it into the bows, picked up my paddle, and pushed away from the rocky shore. My first strokes were vigorous, thrusting the sleek craft into the middle of the lake, then I settled down to my long-distance routine: lift, push down, J-stroke, paddle out, tiny pause for rest, and begin again.

I didn't look back. I didn't see Paddy again, but I had the strangest feeling that I was being watched. I like to think that it was the spirit of Old Alec, standing on Spring Rock and waving farewell.

Epilogue

When I see one robin sitting in a leaf-less tree in early April, I am wont to chuckle loudly and pronounce to the wilderness at large that it is now spring and high time for the last snows to get on with their melting. I don't care if the day is cloudy, or if the temperature is still down in the middle 30's; the robin is here, therefore spring has arrived.

On April 5, 1966, I was paddling against a strong current created by heavy meltwater spilling over the three dams located on the western side of Old Alec's Lake. I had been fighting the flowing water for more than an hour and I had been in the canoe for four hours, ever since I took the red craft from the car's roof rack and launched it into the big marsh.

I had come back to see Paddy and to renew my friendship with Old Alec's Lake, and moments before I sighted the dams as I pushed the canoe up West Creek, I saw the solitary robin perched on a young poplar. The bird sang to me, shuffled its wings, sang again, and flitted to a higher branch, from where it peered down as I passed.

Minutes later I reached South Dam, nosed the canoe against it, disembarked, and pulled the craft out of the water. The robin fluted his call; I stood on the dam, my boots immersed in the spilling water, and I looked over the lake, thinking that it was as though I had never left it last October, as though winter had never been.

Lifting the canoe over the dam and slipping it into the lake, I climbed aboard and paddled to Alec's Point, looking around in hopes of seeing Paddy or one of the other beaver; but they were not about. When I reached the familiar rocky beach and landed, I dragged the canoe ashore quickly and walked to the cabin. It had collapsed even further. There had been much snow this year; it had pulled down a part of the roof and crumbled the south wall. From the cabin I walked to the tent site, noting the depression made by my use of this square of ground; the fireplace was as I had left it, the spring burbled happily, Paddy's old lodge had survived. I returned to the canoe and unpacked, a fairly simple task this time, for I had not come to stay here long, only one week.

I had to come. I spent the long winter months in the city trying hard to rid my mind of the influence that Paddy and Old Alec's Lake exerted on it, yet not able to do so. Every day I thought about affairs at the lake, wondering how Paddy was, what kind of a winter was savaging the land, how the wolf family was making out.

The sudden change from tent to comfortable apartment and the unaccustomed luxuries of city living had been pleasant at first. I had wallowed in the bathtub, gone out to dinner with friends, read a number of my favorite books, caught up with all the news, and then wrote news myself. I was lazy and content for about three weeks.

One morning when the alarm clock went off as usual at seven o'clock, I awoke feeling depressed. I took a shower and it no longer felt *good*; I shaved and was irked by the need to do so; I dressed and found myself irritated at having to make a choice of clothes. I left the apartment with a cup of coffee inside my belly, no breakfast, and when I got to the newsroom and sat at my desk and read the assignment that the city editor had stuffed in my pigeonhole, I could find nothing to excite me: an Englishman had arrived in town with a special compound designed to keep pigeons off the roofs of buildings. I was to interview this man.

I resigned that day, and on March 3 I went to Florida, to the Everglades, at the invitation of the state's Flood Control Department, and I spent some interesting weeks exploring off the beaten track. This was better, but I still kept thinking about Old Alec's Lake, and about Paddy, so that by the time I returned to Canada toward the end of the fourth week of March, I had made up my mind to revisit beaver country. By then, I had been offered another job, and because funds were getting low, I had accepted. This gave me only nine days for my trip.

I knew it was early to go and that I would probably reach the marsh at about the peak of flood, but I went anyway. Now I was standing on Alec's Point once again. For a good ten minutes I watched the lake, which was empty of all life. I pitched the tent and tidied up my gear, once again hanging my packsack on the tree branch; then I kindled a fire and sat before it, drinking coffee and feeling comfortably at home.

Later I had an early supper of bacon and eggs and toast made by spiking the slices of bread on a sharpened willow stick and holding them over the glowing coals. Food had not tasted so good for months.

I went for a walk. I crossed Deer Valley and Blueberry Flats and visited the northern ponds. Spring was trying to settle down, but it had not quite achieved its end; day temperatures went up above freezing and the snow melted in the open places and water was free of ice, but in among the trees mounds of crusted white clung stubbornly to the forest floor. Once, I disturbed a groundhog male who was intent on finding a mate; characteristically, he was wandering far from home in his quest, and when he found himself caught in the open, he sought refuge in a skinny cherry tree, climbing noisily, but with fair agility. Ten feet up he stopped, clinging precariously with his small paws while he eyed me fearfully. I talked to him, giving his tree a wide berth, not wanting to scare the poor beast any more than I already had.

In another place an emaciated white-tailed doe bounded out of a thicket and disappeared into a ravine; she was big with her pregnancy. The deer and the groundhog confirmed spring, even though I didn't see another robin; in fact, none of the other migratory birds had returned yet, but the jays were in good form and filled the forest with their cries, and the chickadees and nuthatches were busy flitting from tree to tree, avidly searching for the awakening insects.

East Pond and West Pond were still partly frozen, thick sheets of ice jamming both dams and keeping back the water that lay brown and turgid on top of the ice cakes floating on the ponds. This was to be expected because the ponds were fed by surface runoff and the current in the water was slow in consequence. It would be another week or so before these water holes were fully opened.

Dusk arrived before six o'clock that evening, bringing the

bite of frost, though the dull skies seemed to be clearing. I sat warming myself by a big fire, glad of my northern parka with its comforting fur-edged hood and my Eskimo-made mukluks, which were lined with caribou hair, the warmest, most comfortable footwear to be had anywhere. There would be a fresh skin of ice in the wet places by morning and the lake runoff would be slowed to a trickle.

For an hour I sat more or less unthinkingly, taking in the mood of the night wilderness, enjoying it despite the cold and feeling happy that I was here. Then my thoughts turned to Old Alec and I remembered a story he had told me about his first year here, when he had delayed leaving in spring and had become marooned until breakup time. He survived reasonably well by eating beaver meat and whatever else he could bring down with his rifle, and he had kept scurvy away by gnawing on the inner bark of poplar trees that he scraped off with a piece of tin, a trick he had learned from his uncle, who in turn had picked it up from the Indians, who, in the old days, would all begin to show signs of scurvy by the end of the long winter. With the inborn knowledge of the wild possessed by all native people, they knew that the rising sap of most trees furnished "medicine," mainly vitamin C, that soon rid them of the painful condition.

For a while I was lost in contemplation of the image of the man, sitting here, as I was now doing more than half a century later, while he waited for the ice to go out so that he could paddle away with his bundles of precious beaver blankets, the "hairy bank notes" that had enabled him to build up a financial stake, just as they had enabled Mother and Alfred to buy their store.

The distant tail slap of a beaver made me jump to my feet and walk to the lake edge, listening. Away from the firelight there was pitch blackness, not even an outline could be seen across the dark water. I thought I heard the ripple of a swimming beaver, but I could not be sure, and presently complete silence settled again over the area. I went back to the fire, smoked one last pipe, and turned in for the night.

The days passed pleasantly enough and I fully enjoyed my return to the lake, but I was disappointed when by the morning of the sixth day I had not seen Paddy; and I was depressed, thinking that he had failed to survive the winter. Twice, the buck visited, staying some distance from shore, but showing his usual curiosity. On the third evening I had seen the beaver that I thought was the female; she had emerged on the surface near the big lodge and had soon disappeared behind Bass Island. She was probably carrying young, another litter of kits that would add to the population of the lake and would probably lead to the departure of the two young ones I had met last year.

I was glum at breakfast that morning; tomorrow I had to leave. I was to start my new job in three days. Contrary to all reason, I had come here expecting to see Paddy again, confident that the kit would come when he realized that I had returned. I had been wrong. When I finished eating I debated leaving that day; it was the sensible thing to do, I told myself; it made no sense to linger beside Old Alec's Lake for another twenty-four hours when I had a great deal to do to get ready for work. I almost convinced myself, but at the last minute I decided to give myself a little more time. If I didn't see Paddy today, I would pack up and leave right after breakfast in the morning.

For something to do I collected my gear, packing most of it in the canoe and covering it with canvas; I kept out the food pack, my cooking utensils, and the bunch of bananas that I had brought especially for Paddy. I would leave them for him on the shore next morning. After packing up I had nothing to do but sit by the fire and wait; I didn't intend to leave camp—I might miss the kit while I was away. The day wore on slowly. The weather moderated and only a touch of frost was evident in the air; the sun was shining strongly out of a vividly blue sky. The day before, a small flock of purple finches had arrived.

At midday several large wedges of Canada geese, flying very high, passed over Old Alec's Lake on their way to their northern breeding grounds, their cries, though faint, clearly audible. A small flock of mallards arrived in the afternoon and settled down near the beaver dams, active and gossipy after their long flight from the south. The bush was awakening to spring.

Came suppertime. I opened a tin of corned beef, toasted some bread, and made coffee; I wasn't in any mood to cook as I watched the sun sink and the gloom of evening beginning to descend on the lake. I had just finished eating and was making the coffee when I heard a small splash near the shore. I put down the coffeepot and looked toward the sound; two feet from shore was a beaver, a small beaver.

"Paddy?"

It was a question more than a call. I voiced it as I reached for the packsack and sought the bunch of bananas. The beaver came all the way out of the water and started walking toward me, hesitantly at first, but moving more surely and quickly when I called again.

"Come, Paddy! I know it's you!"

Indeed it was! He came to me, right up to me. He stood on his back legs, propped ramrod stiff by his wide tail, his front paws pressed against his chest and he *mumbled*. By this time I had already peeled a banana and I bent down and gave it to him. He took it and devoured it.

I sat on the ground, legs spread, holding the other four fruits. Paddy came between my legs, sat down also, and put one paw against my right thigh, reaching forward with his mouth. I gave him another banana, peel and all. While he was eating it I reached slowly forward with my hand and patted his head gently. He looked up at me, but didn't flinch or interrupt his munching. I scratched him behind his ears; he had always enjoyed that. He still did. He tilted his head at an angle, mouth full of unpeeled banana, and he slitted his eyes in ecstasy as he savored the taste of the fruit while giving himself up to the sensual pleasures of my scratching fingers.

He ate three bananas, one after the other, and because I was afraid that any more might harm him, I put the other two back into the packsack. For some minutes Paddy stayed where he was, both paws resting loosely on the palm of my left hand while I continued to caress him with my right. Then he turned, scrambled over my leg, and went to sit near the fire. He began to clean his fur.

I made the coffee, poured myself a mugful, filled and lit my pipe, and sat beside my beaver child with, I am sure, an idiotic grin of pleasure creasing my face. It was a perfect reunion during a perfect evening of spring. I was more than content and I knew that this experience would endure in my memory.

Paddy stayed with me for over two hours, but at last he turned toward the water, paused to look back once, and then slipped quietly into the lake. Soon he submerged.

I left Old Alec's Lake just after sunrise the next morning, putting up the mallards when I landed on South Dam and portaged the canoe. As I drifted downstream, the voice of a robin rose clearly above the sound of rushing water.

A Note About the Author

R. D. Lawrence was born in Vigo, Spain, and was educated in Barcelona and at the London Polytechnical Institute. From 1945 to 1973 he was a journalist, writing for British and Canadian daily newspapers. The author of eight other books about wildlife and ecology, R. D. Lawrence now lives with his wife, Sharon, in Toronto, Ontario.

A Note on the Type

This book was set on the Linotype in Granjon, a type named in compliment to Robert Granjon, type cutter and printer— active from 1523 to 1590 in Antwerp, Lyons, Rome, and Paris. Granjon, the boldest and most original designer of his time, was one of the first to practice the trade of type founder apart from that of printer.

Linotype Granjon was designed by George W. Jones, who based his drawings on a face used by Claude Garamond (1510–1561) in his beautiful French books. Granjon more closely resembles Garamond's own type than does any of the various modern faces that bear his name.

Composed by The Maryland Linotype Composition Company, Inc., Baltimore, Maryland. Printed and bound by American Book–Stratford Press, Saddle Brook, New Jersey.

Typography and binding design by Susan Mitchell.